JUSTICE THAT RESTORES

JUSTICE

THAT RESTORES

CHARLES W.
COLSON

Tyndale House Publishers, Inc.
Wheaton, Illinois

Visit Tyndale's exciting Web site at www.tyndale.com

Justice That Restores

Copyright © 2001 by Prison Fellowship Ministries. All rights reserved.

Cover art copyright © 2000 by Jim Whitmer. All rights reserved.

Author photo by Russ Busby. All rights reserved.

Designed by Julie Chen

Edited by Lynn Vanderzalm

Angel Tree® is a registered trademark of Prison Fellowship Ministries. All rights reserved.

Justice Fellowship® is a registered trademark of Prison Fellowship Ministries. All rights reserved.

Neighbors Who Care® is a registered trademark of Prison Fellowship Ministries. All rights reserved.

MatchPoint® is a registered trademark of Prison Fellowship Ministries. All rights reserved.

Detroit TOP®, an acronym for Transition of Prisoners® is a registered trademark of Prison Fellowship Ministries. All rights reserved.

InnerChange Freedom Initiative™ is a trademark of Prison Fellowship Ministries. All rights reserved.

Unless otherwise indicated, all Scripture quotations are taken from the *Holy Bible,* New International Version®. NIV®. Copyright © 1973, 1978, 1984 by International Bible Society. Used by permission of Zondervan Publishing House. All rights reserved.

Scripture quotations marked NLT are taken from the *Holy Bible,* New Living Translation, copyright © 1996. Used by permission of Tyndale House Publishers, Inc., Wheaton, Illinois 60189. All rights reserved.

Scripture quotations marked RSV are taken from the *Holy Bible,* Revised Standard Version, copyright © 1946, 1952, 1971 by the Division of Christian Education of the National Council of the Churches of Christ in the United States of America, and are used by permission. All rights reserved.

Library of Congress Cataloging-in-Publication Data

Colson, Charles W.
   Justice that restores / Charles W. Colson.
       p. cm.
   Includes bibliographical references.
   ISBN 0-8423-5245-7—ISBN 0-8423-5246-5 (sc)
   1. Restorative justive. 2. Criminal justice, Administration of. I. Title.
   HV8688.C63 2001
   364—dc21   00-053203

Printed in the United States of America

05   04   03   02   01
8   7   6   5   4   3   2   1

CONTENTS

INTRODUCTION

OVER THE LAST fifty years, the history of criminal justice has been marked by ever-growing budgets, massive prison construction, the demonstrated failure of rehabilitation and deterrent theories, stubbornly high recidivism rates that are seemingly impervious to all attempted remedies, and rising crime rates, including particularly frightening increases in juvenile crime.

The best that can be said about this rather dismal picture is that corrections and criminal justice officials (including judges, prosecutors, probation officers, and prison administrators) have waged a valiant effort to correct the problems. I have been greatly impressed with the quality and dedication of men and women in this field. To be sure, the prison system houses people safely, and considering the inherent horrors of incarceration, it does so relatively decently, at least in the United States. But despite the most noble efforts, the evidence makes it abundantly clear: The present system falls woefully short, both in ensuring public safety and in providing a redemptive experience for those caught in its grip.

This, then, is the first premise on which I base much of what follows in these pages: *The criminal justice system, which is absolutely crucial if government is to carry out its first duty—the preservation of order—urgently needs reform.* This means we must think about the goals of criminal justice differently. Instead of the old ideas about rehabilitation and deterrence, now largely discredited, we need to think in radically different terms about a system that *restores* the peace of the community shattered by crime. The term *restorative justice* is a relatively new one; sociologists and criminologists have talked about it only in the last decade or so. But the concepts it embraces are ancient ones indeed, rooted firmly, as I will argue, in Judeo-Christian tradition.

My second premise is equally crucial: *Our ideas and philosophies of criminal justice can no longer be considered in a vacuum.* Developing sound policies for criminal justice requires us to look first at broader questions such as, What is justice? What are the overarching goals of society in ordering right and just relationships and in encouraging virtuous behavior? In short, we must look at what makes a just society and then in that light examine how criminal justice policies can play their role, how they fit into the overall philosophy.

But this means examining the elements and attitudes that constitute our system of justice: the nature of law, our anthropological understanding of human nature, the causes of crime, and the purpose of punitive actions. I will be arguing from the perspective of a biblical worldview and comparing the views of law, anthropology, and punishment embraced by other worldviews, including the dominant secular view.

For convenience of analysis, worldviews can be categorized by the answers each one gives to the great questions philosophers have asked from the beginning: Where did we come from, and who are we? What has gone wrong with the world? Is there a way out? And what can we do to fix it? In the biblical model, these categories are represented by *creation, the Fall, redemption,* and *restoration.*

These four categories underlie the four parts of the book. As we wrestle with these questions, a new and different understanding of two things should emerge: the character of the justice society seeks and how society tries to achieve that justice. What will also emerge is my deep conviction, based on work I did over several years in writing *How Now Shall We Live?* (written with Nancy Pearcey).[1] I believe that the biblical worldview is the only one that provides answers that can produce both personal redemption and a truly just public order.

Note that the case made in these chapters does not come from some abstract philosophical reflection or ivory-tower debate. The case here is based on evidence and experiences gained by working in prisons over the past twenty-five years.

When I was released from prison in 1975, I vowed never to return. I had been special counsel to the president of the United States. Caught up in the biggest scandal in American history, I spent seven months incarcerated for a Watergate offense to which I pled guilty. In prison, I wanted nothing more than to be back home and quietly practicing law.

But God had other things in store for me. I felt a conviction to begin the ministry known today as Prison Fellowship Ministries and Prison Fellowship International, now chartered in eighty-eight countries around the world. In the United States alone, thousands of volunteers are mobilized to visit prisons, conduct Bible studies, lead evangelistic crusades, and provide one-on-one mentoring. Volunteers in a Christmas gift program called Angel Tree reach nearly half a million kids each year, delivering gifts and often establishing relationships. I personally have visited prisons in forty different countries around the world and have looked crime in the eye. I have talked to enough offenders to have a real sense of the wrong moral choices that lead people to crime. I've also seen the utter futility of the prison system. And thousands of times over, I have seen the glorious, transforming power of Christ at work in the lives of the men and women incarcerated, as we will discuss in later chapters.

As Prison Fellowship Ministries developed its strategies, we established a subsidiary known as Justice Fellowship, which works full-time in criminal justice reform, not only advising state legislators and public officials but also working with foreign governments through Prison Fellowship International. My colleagues working in Justice

Fellowship have pioneered the restorative justice model that is laid out in the following chapters.

The Prison Fellowship movement also spawned a subsidiary called Neighbors Who Care that establishes local chapters through which volunteers assist crime victims.

We have been actively involved in questions of restitution and reconciliation as we have worked to rebuild communities from the ground up. We know that restorative justice works, that communities can be recaptured, and that the terrible damage created by crime can be repaired. What you read in the pages that follow has been tested and proven; this is practical stuff that works.

The seeds for this book were sown when I recently prepared material for a series of lectures about criminal justice. I began to realize that the message I was articulating needed broader exposure and that I needed to write a book that would help American policy makers and people who work in our country's criminal justice system to think through their positions, policies, and practices.[2]

Men and women today are discovering the moral bankruptcy that the modern worldview has created. They are looking for something better, a more rational worldview that will lead to a truly just society.

In addition, growing numbers of corrections officials are acknowledging the weaknesses of what have been the prevailing views of penology and criminal justice. They are looking for more effective means of carrying out their very great responsibilities. I hope and pray that they—and you—will find the following arguments persuasive.

It is time for justice that restores.

PART ONE

THE BASIS
FOR A
JUST SOCIETY

CRISIS IN CRIMINAL JUSTICE

WE OFTEN THINK that crime happens only to other people or that honest people, such as clergy, are safe from its effects. This is not always true. Consider, for example, the robbery at the rectory of a Catholic priest in Annandale, Virginia. A break-in occurred in the middle of the night, trapping the priest in his bedroom. According to one report, the priest took his pistol from its box and "ordered the stranger to freeze and lie on the floor." When the intruder didn't stop, the priest was forced to fire his weapon and chased the intruder down the hall. The intruder stopped to confront the priest two more times, and each time the priest fired his weapon—once at the robber's feet and the other "wide of his target." After the third shot, the man fled with a small amount of cash.[1]

In other places the rise of such assaults have provoked some strange responses. Take, for example, the unusual measures some members of the British clergy are taking. Provoked by a series of assaults on its ministers, including the stabbing death of a priest in Liverpool, the Church of England urged its clergy to take preventive measures such as installing panic buttons in their pulpits. Quick to sense an emerging market, Ivan Silversmiths now offers, in both sterling and gold plate, items called "personal security crucifixes." According to the promotional materials, a tug on the crucifix will emit an ear-piercing sound that is audible for 150 yards. The cost is two hundred pounds (around $480), a bit steep, but perhaps reasonable in view of the device's collateral uses: It must be very effective in waking up a somnolent congregation.[2]

Although I don't own a personal security crucifix, I must say that it has captured my imagination because it is at once a sacred sign of the Atonement and a grim sign of the times we live in. As to the latter, the statistics do indeed paint a dismal picture.

SOBERING STATISTICS

Consider the sheer number of people in prisons. When I was incarcerated in 1974, I was one of 218,466 men and women in American prisons. Today, twenty-five years later, there are 1.3 million Americans in federal and state prisons—and another 600,000 in local and county jails. (By the time this book hits the stores, the number is projected to have topped 2 million.) Comparing prisons alone, that is a sixfold increase.[3]

Crime has increased just as dramatically. From 1960 to 1998, crime overall increased nearly 300 percent, violent crime nearly 500 percent.[4] You may have heard that crime rates have dropped recently in the United States. Property crime is indeed down by 32 percent since 1993, and violent crime has dropped 27 percent.[5] But this is not due to some sudden success in criminal justice and penal policies. It is mostly due to demographic factors: The so-called baby boomers, the large cohort of those born in the optimistic years right after World War II, are maturing out of the crime-prone age. Another factor accounting for these trends is the incredible prison-building boom, which has incapacitated a large number of criminals and prevented their continuing to commit crimes—for a time at least. Some of the decrease is also due to the significant spread of more effective approaches to policing and to developing community programs, which will be addressed later. Yet, even after the drop, the total is still extraordinarily high—and most demographic projections suggest that crime is due for another rise as soon as the children of baby boomers reach the crime-prone age groups and as revolving-door prisons graduate new classes of hardened criminals.

The problem is not solved; it will likely only worsen. The recidivism rate remains largely unchanged—around 70 percent—so if there were approximately 200,000 people in prisons in 1974, there were approximately 140,000 repeat offenders; if there are 2 million people in prisons today, we should expect 1,400,000 repeat offenders. The huge prison bulge may temporarily slow down crime, as it apparently has, but as offenders are released, the number of new crimes can be expected to skyrocket.

Most alarming is the fact that much of the increase in crime, particularly violent crimes, has come from juveniles. A growing core of the criminal population is getting younger and meaner. Arrests of juveniles for violent crime grew from 18,165 in 1960 to 74,682 in 1983 and to 123,400 in 1997.[6] Between 1984 and 1994 the number of teen homicides nearly tripled from 800 to 2,300.[7] Despite the fact that the youth murder rate has fallen 39 percent since 1994, a young black man in an American city has a greater chance of being killed by gunfire than if he had been an infantryman in Vietnam.[8]

Even more alarming are the future projections. Children of the baby boomers are entering the crime-prone age groups in record numbers; the juvenile sector of the population will rise 2 percent a year for the next decade.[9] This is an ominous trend when one realizes that among these young men and women is a core of increasingly dangerous and alienated youths—what one criminologist calls the "super-predators."[10] There are more than 800,000 youth gang members in the United States, which means that there are more of them than there are U.S. Marines—and I wouldn't bet that the marines are better armed.[11]

THE CHANGING CHARACTER OF CRIME

But even more chilling than the plain numbers is the changing character of crime. Historically, crimes fit the pattern of a good Sherlock Holmes story. Elementary, Watson: Find the motive, and you will find the criminal. That is no longer the case. Today many crimes are done without motive, unless one considers wanting another kid's jacket a serious motive for murder.[12] The single greatest threat to any society is what we are today witnessing: crimes committed by young men and women without consciences, acts of violence and rebellion that are self-justified and perverse.

Consider just this sample of recent horrors:

- In the spring of 1999, two otherwise normal, middle-class young people, seventeen and eighteen years old, raced through Columbine High School in Littleton, Colorado, executing in cold blood twelve students and one teacher. America was shocked, and remains in shock, at the gruesome display of raw, naked evil. These boys, disciples of Nietzsche and admirers of Hitler, enjoyed killing.

"Do you believe in God?" one shooter asked a girl. When she said yes, he asked why but never gave her a chance to answer. He fired point-blank into her face.

- The Littleton incident, horrid though it was, was but the latest in a series of school killings, all equally senseless. Pearl, Mississippi; West Paducah, Kentucky; and Jonesboro, Arkansas, where two clean-cut kids who looked like "the kids next door" took up positions outside the school, rang the fire alarm, and then took dead aim, as snipers would, gunning down their classmates filing out of the school.

- In Oakland, California, in 1993 a woman was running down the street to escape an attacker, only to be tripped by a bystander. As she lay helpless, her assailant stabbed her brutally—and the crowd kept shouting, "Kill her, kill her."[13] It was murder for the sport and pleasure of the crowd—a regression to the moral sewer into which the Roman Empire fell in the era immediately preceding its collapse.

- Two children, one a ten-year-old and the other an eleven-year-old, admitted dropping a five-year-old from the fourteenth floor window of a Chicago housing project because the five-year-old refused to steal candy.[14]

- Two teenage boys in New Jersey ordered a pizza. When the deliveryman arrived, they killed him in cold blood, leaving the pizzas uneaten and strewn in the snow. "They just wanted to see what it would be like to kill somebody," explained a law enforcement official after interviewing them.[15] Perversely, the idea caught on, and a wave of copycat crimes followed.

- Two New York City teenagers, one from a wealthy family and attending a fashionable school, for no apparent reason killed a stranger walking through Central Park. Then they disemboweled him, disfigured his face, and left him floating in a pond in the park.[16] This is the story so shockingly told in William Golding's modern classic *Lord of the Flies* coming to life in our midst. Could nice, civilized young boys who were products of good schools become mere animals? That was the question. The answer, empirically demonstrated, is that some can and do.

- A few years ago, Melissa Drexler, while attending her high school prom, excused herself from her boyfriend to go to the washroom, where in a few minutes she gave birth to a full-term child. She then straightened out her dress, washed her hands, put the baby in a sack, and dropped him in a trash bin. Rejoining her boyfriend, she asked the orchestra to play her favorite song, which happened to be entitled "Unforgiven." She danced away the rest of the evening, seeming to enjoy herself, classmates reported, and she seemed really surprised when she was arrested.[17] One psychiatrist said of Drexler that to her the baby was simply a foreign object, like a "peach pit."[18]

Examples just as horrid abound among the record 2,300 murders committed in 1994 by American teenagers (up from only 800 a decade earlier).[19]

The horror of all this came home to me in an unforgettable way a few years ago when I visited the Indiana State Penitentiary at Michigan City. It was my fourth visit during a twenty-year span. I walked the cellblocks that day and experienced something I've rarely encountered in the six hundred prisons I've visited around the world: some men refused to come to the bars to speak. Two approached the bars out of curiosity but then refused to shake my outstretched hand. Those who did talk stared at me through the bars—they seemed mere children—with vacant expressions and cold, steely, hard eyes. As I left the cellblock, I put my hand on the shoulder of one man sitting on a chair, only to have him brush it away angrily. I've never seen such hostility.

Then as we assembled in the yard, I saw something I thought I never would see again in America. The black inmates sat on one side of the prison yard, the white inmates on the other. When Mike Singletary, an African-American athlete of some renown, addressed the inmates, only the black inmates responded. When I spoke, only the white ones responded.

When the speeches were over, I turned to the assistant warden, an old friend of mine and a Christian. "This place has changed," I told him.

"Changed?" he replied. "I guess it has. Ten years ago I could talk to these guys about right and wrong. Today they have no idea what I'm talking about."

The assistant warden went on to tell me that in the past the principal administrative problem in prisons had been protecting the younger convicts from the older ones who tended to be predators. Today, he said, the principal administrative problem in prisons is protecting older convicts from the kids coming in off the streets. Other officials have told me the same thing.

We know that all human beings have a conscience, as the apostle Paul tells us in Romans 1 and 2, and yet conscience must be trained; civilized habits and behaviors must be cultivated by moral teaching and discipline. As C. S. Lewis said, "The right defense against false sentiments is to inculcate just sentiments."[20]

The sad conclusion one must draw from the cases I have related, and many, many others, is that we have simply failed in this most basic task of civilizing society through inattention to the moral and spiritual development of our children. The result is a generation with suppressed and deadened consciences. Many of our young people act like savage children, lacking any human characteristic of decency, respect for life, and concern (if not compassion) for others. Many young people see no difference between operating a video game and thrill-killing a pizza deliveryman or a bystander on the street. In fact, video games are similar to military training in one very chilling respect: Both train people to shoot and kill lifelike characters, thereby dismantling the natural human disinclination to kill another human being. The difference, of course, is that soldiers absorb this training in a moral context that also stresses love of country, devotion to comrades, and compassion toward the helpless; video games, on the other hand, and the street culture that they reflect and reinforce, revere none of those values.[21]

This disregard for human life and dignity cannot be dismissed as just another social phenomenon: It is a huge, gaping crack in the foundation of civilized society. It threatens our very survival.

WHAT IS THE REMEDY?

The remedy to this crisis goes far beyond building more prisons, hiring more police, or writing tougher penalties into the law. Such measures, no matter how draconian, will have no effect on consciences or on the culture that trains consciences. Moral failures don't register on metal detectors, and other proposed panaceas such as eliminating poverty and racism, tighter gun controls, better education, or more therapy are nothing but palliatives for the crime problem.

The primary purpose of criminal justice is to preserve order with the minimum infraction of individual liberty. Accomplishing this requires a system of law that people can agree on and that therefore possesses not just power but also authority. It also requires commonly accepted moral standards that serve as voluntary restraints and that inform conscience. Those standards need to express an accepted understanding of what is due to—and required from—each citizen. Finally, criminal justice requires a just means to restore the domestic order as well as a punishment system that is redemptive.

FOUNDATIONAL QUESTIONS

One can quickly see that rethinking criminal justice involves questions far more profound than simply what should be done about sentencing policy or prison construction. One reason our criminal justice system has fallen so short in reducing crime and disorder is precisely that it has not been considered in the broader context of one of the most fundamental questions any society must deal with: What is justice?

I see this question as being inescapably connected with worldview assumptions, with questions about life, ultimate reality, origins, and human purpose. So this extended discussion of criminal justice will lay out four fundamental categories for analyzing worldviews, addressing questions the great philosophers have always wrestled with.

1. Where did we come from, and who are we? Were we purposefully created? Did we merely happen to evolve? Is the human an amalgam of body and soul, depraved because of original sin yet capable of redemption by God? Or are we animate bodies, naturally good, or at least morally neutral until corrupted by society around us, but capable of self-redemption or of redemption by government activism? Each answer leads to its own anthropology with its own implications about how to achieve justice and deal with crime.

2. What has gone wrong with the world? How do we account for the evil that drives men, women, and children to commit crimes? What do we make of evil and suffering—the bad things that happen in our midst? The answers to these questions have profound implications for the basis on which we strive to build a society of law and justice.

3. Is there a way out? Can individuals, as well as cultures and societies, be redeemed? Can we be freed from that which oppresses us? Here the alternatives are as numerous as the various religions and philosophies of the world. Yet, in the final analysis, all the non-Christian alternatives are forced to answer with a resounding no, while the answer of Christianity is a resounding yes. In saying this,

I do not mean to deny that people of other faiths or people who hold to no faith at all can participate in restorative justice programs, implement redemptive policies, or be rebuilders of broken communities and broken lives. They can do all those things—but in so doing, they are "doing a Christian thing," a thing that cannot be fully explained apart from Christianity.

4. *What can we do to fix what has gone wrong?* If there is hope for redemption, how does it apply to problems and consequences of crime? Can the peace of societies ravaged by crime be restored? I believe that there are concrete, empirically tested answers to these questions, and I believe those answers are found in the concept of restorative justice.

In this book I will attempt to answer these four questions in the context of what it takes to create a just society and what kind of criminal justice system is necessary to support it. I suppose I have tipped my hand, so, having reflected on these questions for many years, I shall tell you at the outset my conclusion. Only the biblical worldview can sustain a rational, livable, and just society. No other worldview— be it naturalism, Eastern pantheism, the New Age beliefs, postmodern secularism, liberation theology, or whatever—can escape either its own internal contradictions or disastrous implications that lead to moral and social disarray. No other worldview can create a truly just social order. I hope the material in these pages will persuade you of that. I believe that as we struggle with these issues, we can rebuild a culture of civility and decency out of the chaos of modern life.

WHAT IS JUSTICE?

Before we examine justice in the light of these four worldview categories, we need to address what we mean by *justice*. This is a central question for any society to ask in any era, in any time, because it goes

to the heart of what society is. At the very least, every society wants
to create a just, moral order so that people can live together in
harmony and security. Thomas Hobbes in the seventeenth century
taught that people create civil society by resorting to an omnipotent
government out of fear. But he was wrong. They create it by agreeing
on certain principles of justice. This agreement may be explicit, as in
the case of the Declaration of Independence and the U.S. Constitution
or in the case of the Pilgrims' founding their society in New England
with the Mayflower Compact. Or it may be implicit, as in those societies—such as Britain—that develop many of their standards of
justice through tradition and experience. Either way, some concept
of justice is necessary to unite a society. Any society has to possess
some bedrock agreement on how it is going to arrange its social and
moral relationships and its political structures to ensure that its citizens can live together in some reasonable, safe, and sane way.

A society that is raising questions about how it must order its political social relationships, by what moral principles it is to live—not just
in political theory seminars, but regularly, publicly, and frequently—
is a society in revolution, despite the outward appearance of calm and
continuity. I suggest we are in such a time. Underneath the thin
veneer of the "Era of good feelings," where high stock values and an
everexpanding set of middle-class entitlements seem to anesthetize
most people to the questions of life, those great questions are nonetheless being asked. The media and the political classes anxiously label
such questions "divisive" and hope they will go away. But they won't.
They are foundational, and without finding answers to them, the
foundations will crumble.

The question, What is justice? takes us back to the foundation of
political philosophy. In Plato's *Republic* this question touches off the
whole dialogue. In trying to get at the strengths and weaknesses of
various definitions, Socrates and his young students examined almost

every facet of social life: artisanship and trade, family life, war and peace, and finally the life of the philosopher. I wish I could tell you how they end up answering the justice question. Their conclusions have been hotly debated. After proposing that society be ruled by philosopher-kings, Socrates seemed to discourage his listeners from politics and instead urge them toward the life of philosophy, considered to be something abstracted from politics. (Does he therefore mean that communal, social justice is impossible?) Along the way, he conclusively demolished the belief that justice is nothing more than the interest of the stronger prevailing over the weaker and thus that justice is a sham. He showed that justice is not some shifting, arbitrary cultural construction but an objective, knowable reality. On this foundation, political philosophy was born. On this foundation law rests.

THE FUNDAMENTAL BASIS OF JUSTICE AND THE LAW

ASKING WHAT JUSTICE is requires us to answer the first question in our list of worldview assumptions: Where did we come from, and who are we? Do we live in a divinely created world or in a random, godless one? How we answer these questions determines what I believe to be the first mark of a just society: the rule of law, an objectively true juridical framework for maintaining and assuring just treatment of, and relations among, all citizens. A society has a foundation for justice when it observes a rule of law grounded in objective truth.

At this first, most basic level, there are only two alternatives: Either we are created, and the law is the law because its reference point is the Creator, or this is a godless universe, and the law is merely what humans from time to time decide it is—because there is nothing else for it to be.

All attempts to establish a middle ground between these alternatives have collapsed. Tepid deism either warms up into full-blooded theism or freezes into practical atheism. As Pope John Paul II has noted, even though theoretical atheism is rare today, practical atheism is widespread. Many people who would not deny the existence of God if asked directly about God, nonetheless live their lives as if God does not exist. In the end, deism is not that different from atheism. What does it mean to affirm that God exists if at the same time you affirm that God does not matter?

Looking at the alternatives, we need to ask: Is justice possible in a system of either theoretical or practical atheism? Can a just system for human relationships and social order be achieved in a society in which naturalism is the ruling presupposition? Can naturalism provide a basis for law?

NATURALISM VERSUS THE LAW OF NATURE

Basically, naturalism is the idea that everything arose by chance and is explainable by natural—rather than supernatural—causes. In the Western world, naturalism was a cutting-edge view in the eighteenth century; it took hold of the elites in the nineteenth; and it became utterly dominant in the twentieth. Although today there are some hopeful signs that its hold may be waning, naturalism has profoundly affected modern political philosophy and our jurisprudence.

The Western Tradition

The rise of naturalism represents a radical departure from the longstanding tradition of political and legal thought that had dominated Western culture. That tradition had achieved the seemingly impossible task of synthesizing biblical and nonbiblical sources—Jerusalem and Athens, the world of ancient Israel and the ancient classical republics—into a whole that taught the reality of a personal Creator-God and of a law of nature based on his will and reflecting his holy and righteous character.

This tradition took for granted that God ultimately stood behind the law. There was an ultimate appeal beyond human will. For the Hebrews, law came directly from God. Other ancient Near Eastern cultures, perhaps reflecting the light of natural revelation, had a similar idea about law. For instance, the Babylonians believed that the Code of Hammurabi had been given by the sun god. The Greeks and Romans did not know of God as a unique and omnipotent person. The average Greek believed in the Homeric gods, who were personal but not unique or omnipotent, while some of the more philosophically inclined Greeks believed in a god who was unique and powerful but not personal, not involved in any ongoing fashion with his creation. It was similar with the Romans, except that they added the cult of the household gods, which were specific to each family.

Despite these differences of theology, if one may call it that, we must keep in mind that the Greeks and Romans benefited from the general revelation to which the apostle Paul alludes in Romans 1 and 2: They knew the law that was written on their hearts just because they were human. As we have already seen, Socrates, the great questioner, believed that justice was a thing that really existed, not a mere construct imposed by the powerful. Aristotle investigated right and wrong as if they really existed, and Cicero elaborated on the theory of natural law in a way that was not surpassed until Thomas Aquinas addressed the issue in the thirteenth century. Thus, the ancient world recognized a source of law beyond human will. One can expand the consensus even further by noting that outside the Mediterranean world there was an awareness of a right order of things, what the Chinese called the Tao—an order that mere mortals did not create and that we violate at our peril.

The State as Lord

In the sixteenth and seventeenth centuries, the works of Machiavelli and Thomas Hobbes began to undermine this broad and long-standing consensus. Instead of the divinely ordained natural law—this is naturally right, and that is naturally wrong—Machiavelli substituted the will of "the prince," the man of *virtú*, defined not as Christian virtue but as radical assertiveness and decisiveness. Hobbes, for his part, substituted fear and the will to self-preservation as the driving forces of society, leading people to bestow omnicompetence on an all-powerful "leviathan" state.

But trends giving ultimate power to the state had started even before the Renaissance. King Henry II is viewed as a great law reformer in twelfth-century Britain. There is no denying that his reforms contributed to civic order, and I am sure most people in England were glad to have a little more order after the chaos of Stephen's reign. (People crave order, and they will get it one way or another—a point to which I will refer later.) But Henry's achievement came at a cost: The state—at that time, an institution still in its infancy—got hold of criminal justice.

In the earlier centuries of the Middle Ages, crime had been conceptualized as an offense by one member of the community against another, calling for reparation by the offender to the victim or to the victim's family. This concept arose from the biblical model, which prescribed either capital punishment or, in the case of lesser offenses, injunctions to repay those who had been offended against. This can be seen plainly in early medieval European law codes, which often read like catalogues of body parts, complete with prices in the form of fines for cutting them off—fines that were for the most part payable to the victim or the family, not to the king or the state. But as a result of Henry's zeal to consolidate his authority and to establish "the king's peace" from one end of the kingdom to the other, crime came to be handled in the common law as an offense against the crown, requiring a penalty that need not take any account of the victim. This development profoundly affected the role and outcome of criminal justice for victims and for the community.

Meanwhile, parallel developments were going on in the rest of Europe. The reforming popes of the eleventh century had developed the legal system called canon law. At about the same time, scholars rediscovered the compilations of Roman law made by the Emperor Justinian II in the seventh century A.D. (Justinian failed in his bid to reestablish Roman imperial authority in western Europe; for that reason, knowledge of his code was largely confined to his eastern capital, Constantinople, for half a millennium after it was compiled.) Secular rulers, playing catch-up with the church, used Justinian's codes to develop sophisticated legal systems of their own. This, many historians believe, was the origin of the "state" as we have known it ever since.

By the time Hobbes came along to deny that the citizen had any duty higher than obedience to the state, the state had developed as an institution capable of, and interested in, exercising the scope of power Hobbes envisioned.

This challenge to the great tradition of divinely ordained natural law did not go unanswered. Although both Catholic and Protestant thinkers had their hands full debating each other in the Reformation, some on each side found time to reassert the primacy of God's law over human will. On the Counter-Reformation side, the tradition of natural law as developed by Thomas Aquinas was carried on by both the Dominican and Jesuit orders. On the Reformation side, Samuel Rutherford wrote his *Lex Rex,* or *The Law Is King,* challenging the divine right of kings and asserting the primacy of an objective rule of law. Rutherford's influence on our country's Founders has, I think, been underestimated by historians.

But the main trunk line, so to speak, of Western intellectual history went more in the direction scouted by Machiavelli and Hobbes—a direction that declared God irrelevant to politics and that made the state paramount in the citizen's life. Some blame must go to René Descartes, who was a seventeenth-century philosopher and a Christian (but not a Christian philosopher). Amidst the corrosive skepticism that was becoming dominant in the world of philosophy, Descartes decided philosophy could not start with revelation, or even with sense impressions, but only with that which one absolutely could not doubt. For Descartes, that undoubtable fact was that he himself was engaged in the act of thinking. Because he was thinking, he must exist. This, of course, is the famous formula *cogito ergo sum*. Anything beyond that, Descartes said, must be proved by necessary inferences. With this conclusion, Descartes eliminated any reference point outside the thinking self.

The Enlightenment Influence

Descartes and the philosophers who followed him in what came to be called the Enlightenment believed that there was a vantage point of pure rationality—untainted by religious doctrine, social tradition, or prejudice of any kind—from which they could discover truth. But when they reached this supposedly privileged vantage point, they found not truth but ideology. Having cast aside revelation as a foundation for discerning truth, the Enlightenment became ever more irrationalist. By the time of the French Revolution, the political embodiment of the Enlightenment project, a figure labeled "the goddess Reason," was enthroned in the streets of Paris and in the Cathedral of Notre Dame, but ideological lunacy was building up in the halls of government, culminating in the Reign of Terror, and later, in Napoleon's rule—demonstrating yet again that people demand order and will get it, in good forms or bad.

Jean-Jacques Rousseau provides a key example of the Enlightenment's degeneration from overconfident rationalism into irrational ideology. He rejected the icy, geometric thought world of the early Enlightenment, but he offered instead only dangerous abstractions such as the "general will" and the "social contract." According to Rousseau if we are not yet able to function as the perfect beings we naturally are, it is only because we are still oppressed by the traditional institutions of society and need to replace them with more "rational" ones. Thus was born in the eighteenth century the utopianism that was to cause so much terror in the twentieth century. This utopianism asserted that we can achieve a this-worldly redemption through political action, especially through the seizure and use of power by an enlightened vanguard. The political theories and actions of Marx, Lenin, Mussolini, Hitler, Stalin, and Mao all had roots in the much gentler-sounding Rousseau.

Legal Positivism or Realism?

In the realm of legal theory, the generation following Rousseau saw the rise of legal positivism—the doctrine that there is no objective justice by which law is to be tested. John Austin, the early nineteenth-century English legal theorist generally viewed as the founder of legal positivism, took Hobbes's teaching—about the leviathan state created by social contract out of fear of violence—to its logical extension in the field of jurisprudence. The positivists taught that law is neither more nor less than the command of the sovereign, the will of leviathan. While Austin was gaining influence in England, the Continent saw a parallel development in the rise of Friedrich Karl von Savigny's "historical school," which taught that law develops out of the needs of particular societies in particular times, with no objective, permanent, or transhistorical reference point.

In the United States and in England, legal positivism was slower to take hold. Austin and his school influenced the legal philosophers but not the practicing bar. There are several reasons for this. In both countries, the tradition of the dependence of government on higher law was well represented in certain foundational documents. In England it was the Magna Carta, the groundbreaking charter limiting the arbitrary powers of the king. From that point, if not earlier, to Sir William Blackstone in the eighteenth century, the concept of a higher law undergirded English common law. As Blackstone wrote, echoing Augustine: "The law of nature dictated by God Himself . . . is binding in all countries and at all times. . . . No human laws are of any validity if contrary to this."[1]

Americans enshrined the same truth in the Declaration of Independence, proclaiming that the laws of "Nature and of Nature's God" are "self-evident" and that these include the truth that "all men are created equal, that they are endowed by their Creator with certain unalienable rights."

A glorious example of the endurance of the biblical view and the natural law tradition in the English-speaking world well into the era of the Enlightenment was the stirring eighteenth-century speech given by Edmund Burke to the House of Lords during the impeachment trial of Governor General Warren Hastings of India. The governor general had claimed a right to use arbitrary power to subdue unruly nationals, arguing that they were, after all, used to despotism. Burke replied with these powerful words:

> [The governor general] had arbitrary power? My lords, the East India Company have not arbitrary power to give him. The King has no arbitrary power to give. Neither your Lordships nor the

Commons nor the whole Legislature have arbitrary power to give. . . . We are all born high, as well as low, governors as well as governed, in subjection to one great immutable pre-existing law, a law prior to all our devices and all our conspiracies. . . . This great law does not arise from our combinations and compacts; on the contrary, it gives to them all the sanction they can have. Every good and perfect gift is of God; all power is of God.[2]

Well into the nineteenth century, British and American lawyers still operated on a firm foundation of natural law. But by the late nineteenth century the cutting edge lay with pragmatists such as William James and Josiah Royce as well as their counterparts in the courts and law schools, the legal realists such as Jerome Frank and Oliver Wendell Holmes. Their way of thinking—skeptical, positivist, hostile to Christianity as a worldview, and friendly to it only as an ornament of polite society—has not lost its grip even to this day (except that today even the ornamental value of Christianity is questioned). Most of the justices of the U.S. Supreme Court since the 1920s have been formed in this way of thinking, and very few have had the intellectual independence to transcend it.

The core doctrine of the legal realists was that when judges resolve a case, they are not seeking out objectively existing legal principles and applying them; rather, they are applying their own policy preferences. And, said the legal realists, that's all they *can* apply—preferences—because there *are* no universally valid principles. Judges have nothing to apply other than their mere preferences. Enlightened judges will study contemporary social conditions and judge cases in light of what Oliver Wendell Holmes loftily called "the felt necessities of the time." Less enlightened judges will simply enforce their class prejudices. But, said the legal realists, in either case, there is no objective legal or moral order to guide judges' decisions. The legal realists were philosophical relativists, and relativism—disbelief in objective truth—is the fruit of the Enlightenment's doomed project of attributing truth only to propositions that are as plainly self-evident as Descartes's "I think, therefore I am."

Relativism remains the common language of moral thinking, especially on college campuses. Allan Bloom, at the beginning of his best-seller *The Closing of the American Mind,* observed that "almost every student entering the university believes or says that he believes that truth is relative."[3] Speaking some years ago at the installation of a new president of my alma mater, Brown University, distinguished historian Arthur Schlesinger defended relativism as virtually synonymous with intellectual freedom, warning that "it is the belief in absolutes . . . that is the great enemy today of the life of the mind."[4] This would surely have surprised the Reformation divines who founded our country's great northeastern colleges, including Brown.

In the United States, schools are churning out lawyers who have been immersed in the notions of positivism, legal realism, and relativism. The late nineteenth century saw the rise of law schools as graduate institutions. This has affected aspiring American lawyers in two ways: (1) it means that the positivist and relativist philosophers had a chance to get at them before they came to law school; (2) it means that progressive and liberal legal philosophers could secure teaching positions in the law schools and thus get at the future lawyers.

We cannot take refuge in the comforting myth that relativism is merely a disease of the elites. Pollster George Barna found a few years ago that two-thirds of Americans reject the concept of absolute truth.[5] And here's a stinger for you: Barna found that among people professing to be Bible-believing Christians, the percentage of those rejecting the concept of absolute truth was only slightly lower at 62 percent.[6] Another pollster, George Gallup, found 69 percent support for the statement "There are few moral absolutes: what is right and wrong usually varies from situation to situation."[7]

If the authority of the law rests on the whimsy of humans instead of a higher or natural law, it puts us all in the very tenuous position of being at the mercy of whatever the presiding judge feels.

THE CONSEQUENCES OF
THE RISE OF NATURALISM

SO WHERE DOES this leave us as we return to the first question on
which the law's authority must rest: What is the origin of man and of
laws that order human existence? Sadly, relativism's firm grip on the
modern mind has enthroned naturalism as the culturally dominant
worldview. And when we look to naturalism for an explanation of
origins, there arise alarming consequences for our concept of justice.

AUTHORITY ISSUES

With the rise of progressive attitudes based on a naturalistic view
of law, the foundations of justice were suddenly in jeopardy. First,

naturalism, which rejects established cultural authority, undermines the authority of the law. I use the term *naturalism* here as the broadest expression of the opposite of the God hypothesis, embracing subjectivism and scientism, to mention just two of its progeny. But by definition, the opposite of the God hypothesis—call it what you will—denies any transcendent source of authority for the law. By unfastening the authority of law from its traditional moorings, that authority is set adrift, inviting any number of novel interpretations of law's meaning.

One very fashionable interpretation in our law schools today is a novelty borrowed from the comparative literature departments: deconstructionism. This school of thought was born in France, the product of the writings of Ferdinand de Saussure, Jacques Derrida, and Paul de Man. Language, so the theory goes, is nothing but a social construction, and texts reveal nothing but the social and cultural views of those in power, who are concerned with nothing but advancing their power at the expense of others.

Deconstructionism made the leap from literature to law under the name "critical legal studies," or the "crits," as friend and foe alike call them. Applying deconstruction to law meant not determining what the drafter of a statute meant or how a court interpreted a common-law precedent but rather "unmasking" the underlying "power relationships." Of course, in unmasking the power relationship, the door is open to an alternative power source, for instance, the judge, duly instructed by deconstructionist legal scholars. These include not only radicals but also some of today's leading liberal scholars. For instance, Ronald Dworkin, the legal philosopher who divides his time between Oxford and New York University, borrows freely from deconstructionist theory in describing the interpretive method of his ideal judge, even as he claims to be merely a garden-variety liberal and not a "crit" at all. Thus the law above the law is shoved aside in favor of the judge and professor above the law.

This is the legal manifestation of postmodernism. While the age of reason, or modernism, introduced the idea that truth could be known by reason, with no recourse to revelation, the postmodern era reflects despair as to whether truth can ultimately be known at all. In postmodernism, there can be no absolute truth, only power relationships and social constructs.

It is quite remarkable to look over the intellectual history of the last fifty years and realize that one man saw early on what most of us have only recently realized about the pernicious effects of destroying the objective meaning of words. That man was C. S. Lewis, whom we can now see was the sentry on the forward lines of Western orthodoxy. I think particularly of his memorable essay "Men without Chests," in which he discussed what he called *The Green Book,* a school text by authors whose names he disguised. The authors told the well-known story of Coleridge at a waterfall. Within Coleridge's hearing, two tourists described the waterfall: One said it was "sublime"; the other called it "pretty." Coleridge endorsed the first description and rejected the second. The authors of *The Green Book* said that the first remark, that the waterfall was sublime, was actually a remark about one's feelings, that this was not a reflection of objective reality. The authors contended that one can express only what one feels about what one sees, which Lewis rightly saw as the beginning of the unraveling of culture. His grave concern was that *The Green Book* was planting in young minds the belief that nothing can be known to be objectively true.[1] Lewis was the first to sound the alarm regarding the consequence of relativism—what's true or right for you may not be true or right for me.

DISINTEGRATION OF THE RULE OF LAW

Second, one can readily see what these trends have done to the rule of law. Ultimately, the rule of law requires that law be based on objective truth for it to be reliable to order not only the relationship of the sovereign to the governed but also relationships among individuals. It is authoritative because it is, in fact, the law, not because someone says it is. But if there is no truth, if law is merely subjective, then there is no rule of law, only the will of whoever holds power.

Relativism and its progeny, critical legal studies and the like, have become so entrenched in legal thinking that students are blind to their implications. I discovered this when I lectured at Yale Law School several years ago. I chose what I thought would be a provocative title: "Why Yale Has Destroyed the Rule of Law." I expected a vigorous debate, if not a riot. So ahead of time I consulted my good friend Professor Stephen Carter, a Christian on the Yale Law School faculty. Over dinner at a local campus bistro, I told him what I proposed to say that evening and asked how I should handle the inevitable student protest.

"Protest?" he replied. "You'll get no protest. Students coming to Yale are taught that the law is amoral. They will listen politely, think that you have an interesting perspective, but they will not regard it as an exclusive truth claim.

"They might not even get it," Carter added.

He knew his students well. That night more than five hundred filled Levinson Hall at Yale. Down in front were perhaps a hundred people from the community—mostly Christians, I surmised—and behind them were row after row of students and faculty, notebooks at the ready. During my talk I became increasingly provocative. I saw a lot of note taking going on, but I wasn't getting a rise out of this audience. I assumed they were saving it all for the question period afterward.

Not so. Most of the questions were from the Christian townies down front, and the questions from the students were relatively tame. In fact, I don't think there was even one hostile question. When the evening was over, the students packed up their notebooks and filed peacefully out of the hall. I had just done my best to challenge the metaphysical premises of their entire education, and the only response they could make was to consider my remarks as one view among many. No wonder the motto of their generation is "Whatever." Deconstructionism has effectively suspended the law of noncontradiction. The students were able to think that something could be both true and not true—true for me but not true for them. Relativism has deprived its adherents of even the ability to get upset by an attack on relativism.

This would be bad enough if its harm were confined to causing our elite lawyers to lead morally reptilian lives. But it gets much worse: Those elite law students end up at blue-chip law firms and write briefs that find their way into U.S. Supreme Court decisions; some of those students get to spend a year as clerks on the Supreme Court, where they get to pour their relativism directly into U.S. constitutional law.

LEGAL CHAOS

Relativism thus creates chaos in the law, resulting in what some of us believe to be a constitutional crisis. Courts, emboldened by the weakening of belief in objective restraints on their authority, have in recent years overturned statutes enacted by overwhelming democratic majorities, and they have created new legal principles to justify the sweeping aside of long-settled old ones.

Consider, for instance, the case of *Romer v. Evans* (1996), in which the Court struck down a Colorado constitutional amendment, democratically enacted by the people of that state in a referendum, barring special civil rights protections based on "sexual orientation." The referendum process, which exists in many states, is one of the purest democratic forms that we practice. But Justice Anthony Kennedy, writing for a majority of the Supreme Court, completely ignored the voters' stated purpose—which was simply to prevent sexual orientation from being equated with race for purposes of civil rights laws—and instead claimed to understand their motives better than they did. "Laws of the kind before us," he wrote, "raise the inevitable inference that the disadvantage imposed is born of animosity toward the class of persons affected."[2] In one sentence, the justices branded as presumptively illegal a moral teaching that is long-established and shared by Christians, Jews, Muslims, and people of other faiths. A millennia-old principle of the natural law, enacted into positive law by a democratic majority, was dismissed as inadmissible bigotry by a five-to-four vote of a committee of unaccountable life-tenured judges.

This is, of course, far from the only time the U.S. Supreme Court has created new law in derogation of long-settled constitutional and common-law principles. There was also the string of decisions involving human life, beginning first with the *Griswold* case (1965) and then *Roe v. Wade* (1973). In these cases the Court took it upon itself to "find" in the Constitution an implied right of privacy that overrode the abortion laws, and it attempted to silence the debate—of all fifty states. Sometimes the Court declines an invitation to create a new right, as in a pair of 1997 cases in which the justices refused to recognize a constitutional right to assisted suicide. But even here, social policy rather than law governs; the justices simply determined that America did not need judicial intervention to create a right to assisted suicide—*yet*. The intellectual victory still rests with Oliver Wendell Holmes, who early in the twentieth century taught that law is subject to never-ending development based on sociological need as determined by judges and law professors.

On one issue in particular—abortion—the Court has dug in so deeply to protect this novel right that it has placed at risk the most essential requirement of a self-governing people, namely, their ability to agree on a common good. In the Court's 1992 decision in *Casey v. Planned Parenthood,* where it unexpectedly reaffirmed the landmark *Roe v. Wade* abortion decision, the Court made two moves. First it defined the "privacy" rationale for the abortion right as a "liberty" protected in the Fourteenth Amendment to our Constitution. Then it went further. Justice Kennedy, again speaking for the Court, defined liberty in sweeping, almost Nietzschean terms: "At the heart of liberty," he wrote, "is the right to define one's own concept of existence, of meaning, of the universe, and of the mystery of human life."[3]

As esteemed legal scholar Russell Hittinger of the University of Tulsa has pointed out, the *Casey* autonomy doctrine, taken seriously, would make all laws unconstitutional because all laws have some moral basis at their root and can therefore be said to curb the autonomy of those who are expected to obey them.

The *Casey* doctrine effectively blocks any society-wide dialogue about the common good. Most attempts at conversation about the common good sooner or later degenerate into comparative weighing of various personal rights or freedoms claimed to be rights.

We have no publicly viable concept of the common good, except perhaps as a state of affairs in which individuals have maximum freedom to pursue their private definition of what is good. This means the government can be, at most, what Harvard government professor Michael Sandel calls a "procedural republic."[4] Government acts only as a traffic cop to keep people who are pursuing self-centered goals from bumping into one another.

THE POSTMODERNIST IMPASSE

A relativistic judicial philosophy leads to what Phillip Johnson of the University of California at Berkeley calls the "postmodernist impasse." Any assertion of law's authority—for that matter, any moral proposition—is instantly rebuffed. *Who are you to tell me what to do?* It's what the late Yale Law School professor Arthur Leff called the great barroom riposte, "Sez who?" No one can say who says. And so we are left powerless to deal with the chaos that the absence of authority inevitably creates.

Once again C. S. Lewis was the first to see the dilemma this postmodern view would create: "Either the maxims of traditional morality must be accepted as axioms . . . which neither admit nor require argument to support them . . . or else there are no values at all, what we mistook for values being 'projections' of irrational emotions."[5] Precisely.

But even today, as we sink deeper into the mire, we fail to see the choice that Lewis so clearly articulated nearly half a century ago. I encountered this firsthand when I briefed the editorial board of a major newspaper chain. I was invited to lunch to talk about criminal justice policies, but before the luncheon began, the publisher, a very distinguished pillar of his community, announced to me that he had led the campaign to take the Ten Commandments off the classroom walls in the schools of his community. When I asked him why, he told me it was a matter of tolerance. I replied that the *Lex Divina* was, after all, the root of American law, and, for that matter, the Ten Commandments were revered by Jews and Muslims as well as Christians and were thoroughly respected by Hindus as well. But to no avail. The publisher insisted that tolerance demanded the removal of any religiously motivated commands.

During the lunch, as reporters took notes, the same publisher asked me about recent studies that had shown that over half the students in school stole from one another. "We must find something to do about this dreadful condition," he lamented.

The thought probably occurred to him at the same moment it occurred to me: "How about hanging a sign that says you shall not steal?"

The publisher looked very uncomfortable. But the truth of the matter is, there is a massive cognitive dissonance in America today. The weakening of religious bonds has unleashed a degree of chaos we find insupportable, and yet the enlightenment on which we preen ourselves prevents us from embracing the only possible remedy.

REDUCED TO THE RULE OF MAN

But the final consequence of a naturalistic view of law is the most chilling. In the absence of the rule of law, we are reduced to the rule of men. To some this sounds extreme. After all, the law is still made by the courts. But what is this that we call the law? That depends on the answer to other questions: Is it the law beyond the law? Is it the democratically enacted law of the people, or is it what judges arbitrarily say it is? Do judges see law as binding and objectively true, or do they see it as a social construct? Do they see their task as interpretation or as the "unmasking" of "power relationships"?

As we slide ever closer to the latter answer and away from the understanding of the law being based on external authority, the law comes to be understood as law *only* because certain human beings say it is—with no recourse should their judgment be arbitrary. And that end result is not liberation, as advocates of relativism promise us, but tyranny.

C. S. Lewis, again, was the one who saw it. "The very idea of freedom presupposes some objective moral law, which overarches rulers and ruled alike. Subjectivism about values is eternally incompatible with democracy. . . . Unless we return to the crude and nursery-like belief in objective values, we perish."[6]

I believe it is demonstrable—and tragically will become more so as time passes—that naturalism's erosion of the law's objective authority in time can lead only to chaos and tyranny, and that only the Judeo-Christian understanding, or the understanding of the natural law (which historically flows from revelation), can assure us of a system of law that provides true justice.

THE IMPLICATIONS FOR
CRIMINAL JUSTICE

BUT, YOU MAY ASK, what does this discussion about the consequences of naturalism have to do with the criminal justice system and
with restorative justice, the more specific focus at hand? My answer
is *everything*.

First, when the law loses authority, it no longer enjoys public
respect. The attitudes of rebellious lawbreakers pervade the culture.
Surely this is one reason for the evident rise in ethical failure both in
government and in private endeavors in recent decades.

We have seen a rash of cases involving jury nullification. A black
jury, for instance, may refuse to convict a black defendant on the

grounds that blacks for years have been oppressed by whites. The facts of racism are all too real, but to deploy them in this way is deconstructionism in its purest form: Justice is reduced to power relationships between groups. What matters is not law and facts in the case at hand, but how the law has been used to mask power.

Britain saw an example of how the law is used as a mask for power with the mass release of terrorists from both sides of the Irish conflict under the 1998 Good Friday Agreement. Many, I understand, saw that as an example not of "justice" but of power relationships between collective entities.[1] People duly convicted of grave crimes were released, not to exact justice, but to achieve a politically concluded adjustment of power between an "us" and a "them."

Yet another consideration is whether a subjective system of law can assure any certainty of punishment or fairness in sentencing. I can tell you, as one who has been in prison, that sentence disparity is one of the chief causes of bitterness among sentenced convicts. If the law lacks objective standards, such disparities can only increase.

British academic lawyer and criminologist Jonathan Burnside of the Relationships Foundation lucidly states that it is impossible to sentence objectively, to create fairness in sentencing, or to inspire public confidence when there is simply no objective ground for preferring one thing or another.[2] And Burnside contends that this makes the justification for a prison sentence vulnerable to political pressure, one reason the prison population has risen so sharply even as the number of indictments has fallen.

Second, it is clear that if the law lacks moral authority, it cannot be a moral teacher. Thomas Aquinas said that without a moral consensus there can be no law. Historically the law reflects the moral traditions and customs of people infused with the spirit of Christ. Historically we have looked to the law for moral guidance, but if the law is merely subjective, it can provide no moral guidance. And if the purpose of law is simply to protect our autonomy, as the 1992 *Casey v. Planned Parenthood* U.S. Supreme Court decision teaches, then the only guidance is that the individual is free to do what he or she chooses, furthering society's tendency to scoff at the law.

Third, under relativist assumptions there is simply no basis in the law to provide baseline standards of justice. The experience of the Russian and Third World economies, with their corrupt governments and crony capitalism, teaches that economies won't work unless they have a strong juridical system that not only protects commercial transactions and property rights but also punishes wrongdoing—where wrongdoing is defined not as the acts of those who happen to be out of power but as the breaking of objective law.

Human rights cannot be justified in a relativist system. What is a human rights claim if not a claim that a higher, objective law takes precedence over what seems expedient to a particular government at a particular time, as Edmund Burke put it so eloquently in the Warren Hastings impeachment trial of 1788? Take the objective higher law off the table, and no government has any reason not to treat people as it chooses. Governments will accord rights only to groups that have political power. In a relativist system, the rhetoric of human rights may survive, but only as a cloak for demands for power.

Without the rule of law, we cannot reclaim what Augustine called the *tranquillitas ordinis*, the peace of the community, which is a crucial reflection of biblical order and justice, as I will argue later. This essential peace in the community is imperiled if there is not an objective standard of justice, and without a reasonable standard, the tranquillity of order can never be restored once it is disrupted.

Finally, if order fails, only strong government can restore it. Given a choice between order and freedom, people always choose order. Out of the chaos that the postmodern interpretation of law has created comes an ever-increasing demand for greater governmental power. It would be the supreme irony if the definition of liberty in the *Casey* Supreme Court decision—that the Constitution protects the utmost individual autonomy—were to create such disorder that people would become so determined to have order that they would be willing, even eager, to sacrifice their liberty.

WHAT MUST WE DO?

The first task in approaching any problem of the magnitude of criminal justice is at least to be able to diagnose the problem. Sometimes when I talk about cases and legal philosophy, I notice some eyes in the audience glazing over. But it is crucial that Christians and thoughtful citizens understand the underlying philosophical issues that are at play in the culture wars and the cases that have resulted from them. It is encouraging to me that lawyers now are increasingly debating these issues. Christian lawyers are sufficiently concerned and are taking steps to strengthen law schools.

Furthermore, some Christian lawyers are becoming aggressive in public advocacy. Every week I receive speeches written by lawyers and judges echoing the themes I have been writing about. There is a growing awareness of the depth of the problem and of its potential consequences.

Not every Christian should be a lawyer (that there would be such a thing at all is in the minds of some an oxymoron), but every Christian should be an apologist, an intellectual defender of the faith. The apostle Peter commanded this: "Always be prepared to make a defense to any one who calls you to account for the hope that is in you" (1 Peter 3:15, RSV). We need to understand the problem and equip ourselves with the arguments in defense of the older tradition of the law— older, dying, yet due for a rebirth. We have a strong case to make as we compare worldviews—sterile naturalism versus natural law, which is a pattern of laws ordered by the Creator.

It should become obvious that only a biblical worldview can produce true justice. For justice is impossible without the rule of law; and the rule of law is impossible without transcendent authority. Legal systems of the past, seeking to implement a divinely authorized rule of law, were sometimes crude, corrupt, or even cruel. But the problem was with the implementers, not with the law they were implementing; human beings have always been and will always be imperfect. Today we have the same fallible human beings administering meaningless, standardless law—and we are worse off, not better.

If restorative justice is to prevail, the first task ahead of us is to restore the authority of the law itself. Without it, no criminal justice system can be fairly administered. Without it, no society can survive.

PART TWO

THE ROOTS
OF CRIME

DEPRIVATION OR DEPRAVITY?

IN PART 1 I raised several questions, among them these two: What is justice, and what is the authority of law in a just order? In part 2 we will turn to equally fundamental questions: What is humanity, and why are we in such a mess? Just as it is often said that a wrong anthropology inevitably leads to wrong theology, so, too, if we have a wrong anthropology, we cannot escape serious mistakes in our ideas about justice.

In the area of criminal justice, for example, the most significant harm wrought by the Enlightenment in displacing the Christian worldview was that of saddling us with a view of humankind that was not only wrong but wrong in such a way as to guarantee us centuries of ineffective law enforcement, with all the human suffering that involves. Most of the failed and flawed criminal justice policies of this past century, to which the high crime rates and burgeoning prison systems stand as towering monuments, can be traced to a wrong view of human nature, a wrong answer to the second great worldview question: What has gone wrong with the world?

GOVERNMENT'S FIRST TASK

A central requirement for a just society is the rule of law. But equally essential is the preservation of order. From the beginning of creation through the establishment of God's covenant and law, the Bible emphasizes right order. Humans were not meant to live in chaos, which is an inevitable consequence of the Fall. So it is the task of individuals and the structures of society—such as families, community groups, and, of course, government—to pursue and preserve order.

Indeed, in the biblical view, preserving order is the first task of government; the angel with the flaming sword stationed at Eden was the first appointed police officer. Note also that in the New Testament the apostle Paul specifically notes that God has assigned the power of the sword to government: "[The person in authority] is God's servant to do you good. But if you do wrong, be afraid, for he does not bear the sword for nothing. He is God's servant, an agent of wrath to bring punishment on the wrongdoer" (Romans 13:4). Augustine later argued that the primary function of law is to restrain sin and promote order.

Indeed it might be said that before a society can reflect God's righteousness, it must reflect God's order. This is not a matter of exalting order over righteousness; it is merely pointing out that you have to build the first floor before you can build the second floor.

And we should not be utopian about government's ability to restrain sin; its ability is, of course, limited. Nonetheless, we are to work to make it as effective as possible.

TWO VIEWS OF HUMAN NATURE

But to say that the law should reflect God's order and that government serves to restrain sin is to presuppose sin. And it is precisely on this point that the two great worldviews—secular naturalism and biblical theism—clash most dramatically. They represent utterly antithetical viewpoints and lead to dramatically different understandings of how government should function to preserve order and promote justice.

The Biblical View

Christians believe in the doctrine of original sin. This is not, as moderns have made it out to be, some dark, repressive, dour view of life. Quite to the contrary, the doctrine reflects God's high view of human dignity (and his gracious provision when we do sin).

The biblical worldview teaches that God created the universe and everything in it. The very pinnacle of this creation is the human being made in the very image of God. God made humans to be holy and to live by his commands so that they would enjoy a full and abundant life. Yet God loved us so much that he imparted to us the dignity of being free moral agents, creatures with the ability to makes choices, to choose either good (that is, to obey him) or evil (that is, to refuse to obey him).

Having given us a free will, a capacity for choice, God provided one moral restriction on our first ancestors, forbidding them to eat of the tree of the knowledge of good and evil. These same first ancestors rejected the good, disobeyed God, and not only marred their relationship with God but also opened the world to death and evil.

The theological term for this tragedy is *the Fall,* and since, according to Scripture, Adam is the federal head of the human race, "In Adam's fall, we sinned all," as the old grammar-school primer expressed it.

The Bible thus puts responsibility for sin squarely on the shoulders of the human race. In that original choice to disobey God, human nature became morally distorted and bent so that from then on, humanity has had a natural inclination to do wrong. (As G. K. Chesterton once quipped, the doctrine of original sin is the only doctrine empirically validated by thousands of years of human history.) Original sin haunts humanity to this day as we act out rebellion against God in a host of ways both as individuals and as social collectives. Once we disobey God, we can repent, but we can't go on as if nothing has changed. As theologian Edward T. Oakes writes: "On its own terms, the doctrine [of original sin] stands as a cipher pointing to what everyone senses in his or her own heart: that sin after Adam always takes the form of *acquiescence* and not origination. We are born, that is, into a world where rebellion against God has already taken place, and the drift of it sweeps us along."[1]

The problem with this answer is not that people find it unclear but that they find it unpalatable; it implicates each one of us in the sin and evil we find around us. But Christians can take heart because just as sin entered the world through one man, so redemption has come to us as well through one man (see Romans 5:12-21). But taking heart from this fact means first of all taking stock of the reality of sin.

If one wants to reject the doctrine that humans were created good but fell into sin, the alternative that best accounts for the facts would be that people do wrong not as the result of a primordial bad choice but simply because we are bad creatures. This is actually a much more pessimistic and antihumanistic view than the Christian one. John Henry Newman put the alternatives starkly and memorably in his *Apologia Pro Vita Sua.* Surveying the many manifestations of human misery, Newman asks: "What shall be said to this heart-piercing, reason-bewildering fact? I can only answer, that either there is no Creator, or this living society of men is in a true sense discarded from his presence."[2]

The doctrine of original sin, which holds individuals morally accountable for their behavior, largely informed Western thought and influenced Western structures and justice policies until the Enlightenment. But the influence of the doctrine of original sin began to unravel in the middle of the eighteenth century, due in no small part to the writings of the young Swiss-born philosopher Jean-Jacques Rousseau, who entered the Parisian intellectual scene advancing the radical idea that the progress of civilization had not been beneficial for human beings but harmful. Rousseau argued that human nature is good in its natural state; people become evil only when they are corrupted by society. His most influential work, *The Social Contract,* opens with the famous line, "Man is born free and is everywhere in chains."[3]

Rousseau's theories became wildly popular and eventually led to the belief that the state would be the ultimate liberator—throwing off all of those oppressive institutions that had put humans in chains. Many enlightened philosophers more or less openly viewed Christianity as one of those ancient and oppressive institutions. The Enlightenment thinker Diderot, for instance, openly looked forward to the day when we would "strangle the last king with the guts of the last priest."[4]

The Secular View

Thus the modern view—what I call the great myth of the Enlightenment, that human nature is good and getting better—emerged as the principal challenge to the historic Christian view of original sin. In the nineteenth century, this encouraged the rise of utopianism. Several

streams of intellectual thought flowed together to make utopianism
a powerful force in modern life. Hegel's philosophy, for one, led to
near deification of the state, which proved to be dangerous indeed,
as traditions that could have acted as constraints on the uses of state
power were being swept away. Darwin and his popularizers in effect
introduced a new creation story for the origins of the world and its
species, one that essentially dispensed with God. And John Dewey,
a very influential American philosopher of the twentieth century,
looked forward to a utopian future in a powerful central superstate
that would establish a new religion of progress, with public schools
as its centers for mandatory catechesis. Like Hegel, Dewey believed
that moral failure would be cured by education, that knowledge must
inevitably result in virtue.

If such utopianism were merely a parlor game, we could ignore it.
But it has had profound effects. Once the notion was accepted that
human beings are by nature purely good—or if not purely good,
perfectible by education or political change—then the way was open
for that uniquely modern form of tyranny, the idealistic kind, built
on notions of human or social perfectibility. The tyrant who knows
he is merely serving his own ends is bad enough, but at least his evil
is limited by his appetites. The tyrant who thinks he is selflessly
trying to improve you and me is without limits because you and I will
never be good enough for him. He justifies the purge of all unhealthy
influences.

Thus we get such paradoxes as the Reign of Terror in the French
Revolution's pursuit of liberty, equality, and fraternity; we get
Marx's nineteenth-century attempts to cure social ills with economic
solutions, which led to the gulags and the killing fields of the twentieth century. (Pol Pot was known to have read Rousseau as he
dispatched 1.7 million Cambodians to be executed.)[5] Fascism also
fits into this paradigm. Although it differs from communism by

consciously drawing on premodern themes (ancient Rome in Mussolini's case, German tribalism in Hitler's), facism was really a very modern attempt to create a state-managed utopia for those deemed worthy of living in it.

The lesson is clear: By abandoning the view that all people are sinful—and, in particular, by rejecting the Christian doctrine of original sin—we have invited tyranny. As French satirist Anatole France is reported to have said: Never have so many been murdered in the name of a doctrine as in the name of the principle that human beings are naturally good.[6]

UTOPIANISM AND MODERN CRIMINAL JUSTICE

A quick survey of nineteenth- and twentieth-century theories of criminal behavior and criminal justice reveals how profoundly our thinking about criminal justice has been affected by the demise of the doctrine of original sin and the emergence of this modern utopianism.

In the late eighteenth and nineteenth centuries, for example, three social thinkers of the utilitarian movement—Cesare Beccaria, Jeremy Bentham, and John Howard—developed criminological theories based on the assumption that criminal offenders are rational calculators who simply choose crime because it offers more benefits than liabilities.

It was the doctrine of free will run amok. The utilitarians rightly believed that people make choices about their actions. But they went on to speculate that people make circumstantial choices by simply weighing pleasure and pain, risks and rewards. This thinking led to the criminal justice principle that for every possible crime there is a level of severity and certainty of punishment that will deter it. Find those levels, and crime can be eliminated. Criminal justice began to look like a pure science.

Biologists, too, developed theories to help explain and address problem behaviors such as crime. For example, Cesare Lombroso, an Italian who lived into the twentieth century, tried to identify biologically criminal "types." In short, he posited that one could tell a criminal by certain physical features. A lot of people still believe this, by the way. Social theorist Enrico Ferri looked to the inter-connections among personal, social, economic, and political factors to explain criminal behavior. Believing that social structures are an important qualifying feature in holding individuals responsible for their actions, Ferri looked to social engineering for a solution to crime. Ferri called for criminal justice and policy to be directed by scientific experts rather than by judges, legislatures, or legal tradition. The experts, Ferri reasoned, would better understand the problem and implement solutions. Thus he was a prophet of what C. S. Lewis later denounced as the "humanitarian theory of punishment," in which offenders are treated more like lab animals than human beings.[7]

Yet a third influential Italian criminologist of the early twentieth century, Raffaele Garofalo, took a step back toward something resem-bling natural law; he believed that there were such things as natural crimes, which no society could refrain from punishing. Regrettably, though, he defined criminals not as people who made decisions to violate the natural law but as people with a glitch in their genetic makeup, which caused them to lack the altruistic sentiments that make people obey the natural law. Because criminals amounted to dangerous evolutionary failures, capable of transmitting their deficiencies to future generations, Garofalo called for them to be eliminated—culled from the herd either through execution (for those who committed the graver crimes) or through life imprisonment or exile. Needless to add, for Garofalo and Ferri, the whole process of sorting out the more dangerous from the less dangerous and imposing appropriate sanctions was a matter for scientific experts, not for ordinary people, their representatives, or their traditions.

One thing can be said for Garofalo: His views led to the conclusion that prisons could merely incapacitate, not rehabilitate. This, at least, he got right.

But not so with Sigmund Freud and the penal reformers he influenced. Freud taught that crime was simply the result of an incomplete process of repressing primal urges. From that assumption Freud concluded that psychotherapy could lead to reform. This view continues to be dangerously influential today.

Meanwhile, Ferri's social-science approach was taken up by "progressives." Today we tend to associate the term "Chicago school" with conservative economics, but in the early twentieth century it meant left-leaning sociology. Chicago-school criminologists such as Edwin H. Sutherland argued that crime is a learned behavior arising from the social environment. Society gets the crime it deserves, they argued, because social structures create crime. Echoes of Rousseau. Thus was established the society-made-them-do-it school that still persists today.

Modern liberalism regards crime as the outcome of impersonal forces in society and therefore relocates responsibility outside the criminal. Clarence Darrow, the lawyer who achieved such notoriety in defending Darwinism in the Scopes trial, was in the vanguard of the belief that criminals were helpless victims of their circumstances. In 1902, in a widely publicized speech to prisoners in Chicago's Cook County jail, Darrow declared: "There is no such thing as a crime as the word is generally understood. . . . I do not believe that people are in jail because they deserve to be. They are in jail simply because they cannot avoid it on account of circumstances which are entirely beyond their control, and for which they are in no way responsible."[8] Darrow's views reflected what became the dominant attitude toward criminal justice for at least the first seventy years of the twentieth century.

A thread of utopianism twists throughout all modern theories. Take the conventional liberal approach. Reformers argued that if offenders (victims, as they saw them) were taken from their unhealthy communities, placed in wholesome environments, and given good examples and counseling, they would cease committing crimes. It was called "resocializing" in the 1930s and 1940s. Prisons were called "reformatories" or "correctional" institutions—names that many of them still cling to. Needless to say, very few people got reformed, but the name stuck as being more pleasant to the ear than the more honest terms *jail* and *prison*.

The sociological Chicago-school variant of utopianism had achieved establishment status by the 1960s, when then-Attorney General Ramsey Clark said bluntly, *poverty is the cause of crime.* Hand in hand with this approach to crime went the view that poverty was caused by inadequate welfare checks or by deficiencies in social services. The cries arose: fund those services, and increase those checks; then poverty will disappear, and then crime will disappear. Needless to say, it didn't work out that way. But that's not to say the Clark doctrine had no impact: It told millions of people of all races in our inner cities that they weren't responsible for their behavior. They were merely victims of poverty; crime was simply a product of that poverty, and therefore it was excusable. That belief profoundly influenced the next generation, with devastating consequences.

Former President Jimmy Carter echoed the same perspective when, during his term in office, a power outage occurred in New York City and widespread looting took place. President Carter declared it was poverty that had driven people to loot. Yet a few months later, studies showed that most of the looters had been employed at the time and that many of the things they stole were things they didn't need and couldn't use.[9]

No one would doubt that efforts to rehabilitate those engaged in antisocial behavior were well intentioned. The people involved took a caring and compassionate approach, and they really believed they could succeed.

Ramsey Clark elaborated on his simple statement that poverty is the cause of crime by describing the "dehumanizing" effect on the individual of "slums, racism, ignorance and violence, of corruption and impotence to fulfill rights, of poverty and unemployment and idleness, of generations of malnutrition . . ." and on and on. But astonishingly, having recited a long litany of horrors, Clark concluded optimistically: "They could be controlled."[10]

But, in fact, these policies simply validated the law of unintended consequences. They not only didn't solve the problem, they compounded it. Despite many attempts to "treat" criminals through a myriad of rehabilitative programs, recidivism statistics showed no improvement. So by the early 1970s, all but the diehard behavior modificationists had begun to despair of the rehabilitative model. The vast majority of correctional officials were by then abandoning rehabilitation as the principal justification or goal of institutionalizing offenders for the simple reason that it just wasn't working. In 1973 the U.S. National Advisory Commission on Criminal Justice Standards and Goals acknowledged: "The failure of major institutions to reduce crimes is incontestable. Recidivism rates are notoriously high, institutions do succeed in punishing, but they do not deter. . . . They make successful reintegration in the community unlikely. They change the committed offender, but the change is more likely to be more negative than positive."[11]

Even governments engaged in extensive prison-building programs recognized the futility of doing so. A special subcommittee in the Canadian Parliament in 1977 concluded in its report, "Society has spent millions of dollars over the years to create and maintain the proven failure of prisons. Incarceration has failed in its two essential purposes—correcting the offender and providing permanent protection to society. The recidivist rate of up to 80 percent is the evidence of both."[12]

But the consequences of treating offenders as victims went beyond prison walls. The people in urban areas believed what they were told by the politicians. Poverty was soon seen as an excuse, then a justification, for crime. Expanding welfare programs began to weaken family structures. Fathers didn't feel responsible for their families. As a result, more welfare was needed, which in turn further entrenched the dependency culture. Young people, increasing numbers of them fatherless or with transient parental models, headed into gangs. Crime exploded, urban areas becoming combat zones. By the early 1990s, violent crime had risen almost 600 percent in America in thirty years (1960–1992). This fueled the greatest boom in prison construction in Western history.

Why didn't someone call a halt? Two reasons.

The first reason was both economic and political. This was illustrated during a national television interview in the late 1970s. I was one of the guests; the other was the corrections commissioner of a large state. During the program I talked about the futility of further prison construction, how prisons were not rehabilitating, how alternatives must be sought and implemented. The corrections commissioner fought every inch of the way, arguing for rehabilitation (which I knew he didn't believe in because he had told me so before we went on the air), and warned of grave dangers to public safety if the prisons were not built.

When the program was over, I asked him why he had so stubbornly defended rehabilitation. He said, "If the public thought it wasn't working, we wouldn't get support for our bond issues to build prisons, and it's time we overhauled our system."

The second reason involved a profound shift in criminology—of which I was very much a part. I mentioned earlier that the errors of Enlightenment and post-Enlightenment thought about human nature had manifested themselves on the political right as well as the left. I know that is true. In the late 1960s and early 1970s, I wrote speeches for Richard Nixon when he was both a candidate and president. These speeches persuaded people that the solution to crime was to get tough, impose long sentences, appoint "hanging judges," free the police from constitutional restraints, and the like. The crowds loved such talk. The theory was that even though prisons didn't rehabilitate, if we could get tough enough, we would discourage crime. The emphasis thus shifted to deterrence, and the prison-building boom continued even more enthusiastically.

In retrospect, this was pure Benthamism, characterizing criminals as rational calculators who would measure the length of prison sentences and the likelihood of getting caught and convicted, against the perceived benefits of committing a crime. It didn't work any more than did the Ramsey Clark poverty-causes-crime school of thought.

One memorable illustration of the failure of what I might call the right-wing Benthamite deterrent approach to crime came from an award-winning TV program filmed in a prison in Rahway, New Jersey, in the late 1970s. Called "Scared Straight," it showed young kids, first- or second-time juvenile offenders, being escorted into the prison cells of the grim, old New Jersey state penitentiary. There a panel of convicts awaited them, most of them serving life terms, and surely chosen by central casting to be the meanest, toughest, most frightening lot of convicts that could be found anywhere. For one hour these convicts literally scared the wits out of the young offenders, shouting at them, threatening rape if they were brought into that prison, and describing prison life in the most terrifying terms. There were horror-stricken expressions on the faces of the boys who later were solemnly escorted out of the prison.

Most people were certain, of course, that this would be the ultimate deterrent to crime. Let these kids see what prison life was like and get a taste of how they would be brutalized, and they would surely go back to their studies and behave themselves like model children. But to almost everyone's surprise, the results were exactly the opposite. The kids who participated in the program turned out to have a higher incarceration rate than those who did not.[13]

Yes, economic calculation and social structures play a role in human decision making, and fear can have some effect, but it's not the whole of it. That's because our natures are affected by sin, precisely as Christians contend. The apostle Paul explains vividly in Romans 7:19: "For what I do is not the good I want to do; no, the evil I do not want to do—this I keep on doing." Because of our sinful natures, we are constantly doing wrong even when we want to do right. The principal deterrents to bad behavior are conscience, custom, and the threat of censure. But when traditional restraints fail, law becomes essential. As sociologist and criminologist James Q. Wilson puts it: "If familial and traditional restraints on wrongful behavior are eroded, it becomes necessary to increase the legal restraints. But the enlarged spirit of freedom and the heightened suspicion of the state [make] it difficult or impossible to use the criminal-justice system to achieve what custom and morality once produced."[14]

If the liberal approach of the 1950s and 1960s was a failure, so too was the conservative approach so enthusiastically embraced in both the 1970s and 1980s. In some respects the conservative approach has been more of a failure, for we continue to build more institutions that have already proven to be failures. The recidivism rate remains stubbornly high. So the more people we've put in prison, the more recidivists come out the other end and turn to more crime.

The result of both approaches has been rapidly escalating crime rates (despite recent and, I would argue, temporary declines) and staggeringly high prison populations. When I was released from prison in 1975, there were 240,600 people in U.S. prisons.[15] Today our prisons and jails house 1.9 million people, and we enjoy, if that is the correct word for it, the second highest rate of incarceration per capita in the world—at the staggering cost of more than $30 billion per year.[16]

We have, in fact, created the prison leviathan—the building of more and more prisons and the emergence of "corrections" as a self-perpetuating industry with a powerful lobby. But this is simply the natural consequence of the trends in modern thinking that I have been describing. Whether you think that human nature is malleable and people are basically good or that people are nothing but rational calculators of pleasure, pain, and risk, the outcome will be prison construction. The human malleability advocates want "reformatories" to experiment with turning bad guys into good guys; the rational calculation proponents want mean, scary prisons, so as to deter. Both groups want prisons.

And the leviathan continues to grow. The *New York Times* reported this year that a new jail or prison is completed at an average rate of about one per week. Our jail and prison population has quadrupled since 1980. In the past two decades, roughly 1,000 prisons and jails have been built. Today American prisons are more overcrowded than when the building spree began, and the inmate population continues to increase by 50,000 to 80,000 people a year.[17] As of the middle of 1998, 1 in every 155 Americans was incarcerated.[18]

We do need prisons to incapacitate those who cannot safely be loosed on society. But that's the only thing prisons are good at. Prison construction, beyond what is needed for the incapacitation function, puts us into a vicious cycle. Our recidivism rate is running about 70 percent. (Although I think this is conservative. I sometimes ask prisoners whether they plan on committing crimes and returning to prison once they're out; naturally, they say no. Then I ask if they were in at least once before; *almost all* say yes. Well, when they were in the first time, you can bet they weren't planning to come back—yet they did.) More prisons feed more recidivism, which in turn feeds the perceived need for more prisons—and so it goes.

William Temple, archbishop of Canterbury during World War II, foresaw the direction penology was going. In his 1934 book, *The Ethics of Penal Action,* he argued that retribution, deterrence, and reform have to be balanced, with none of the three being allowed to dominate penal policy. Retribution alone is mere vengeance. Deterrence, though welcome, is unjust if it is not subordinated to the offender's actual moral desert. And reform of offenders, while "valuable in the sympathy which it exhibits and in the effects which it produces," must respect their freedom as moral agents.[19] (I will have more to say about this in later chapters.)

The rather tragic history of modern criminology I've laid out here reveals that both the liberal and the conservative approaches have failed because both of them are premised on a flawed understanding of human nature. If we reject innate human sinfulness—that dark-sounding Christian view of original sin—we are left with the empty hope that people in their goodness will, if other influences are removed, do the right thing. This feeds the utopian pretension that we can put individuals in institutions and rehabilitate them—that is, make them fit for civilized life—or we can so frighten them by the horrors of prison that they will forever go straight. The record of the last five decades should convince even the skeptic that only the biblical view of human nature conforms to reality. It is the only workable and rational way in which we can look at human behavior and thereby enable law and government to perform their more basic tasks of restraining sin and promoting order.

THE CONSEQUENCES OF
UTOPIAN NOTIONS OF
CRIMINAL JUSTICE

THE CONSEQUENCES of the flawed policies of the utopian
models of criminal justice have gone far beyond the massive prison-
building programs and soaring crime rates I have described. They
have shaped the very character of our culture, with consequences
felt across the board. Let's look at four areas that have been
profoundly affected: the erosion of personal responsibility, the
coarsening of crimes, the dehumanization of the individual, and
the compounding of evil.

EROSION OF PERSONAL RESPONSIBILITY

First, in denying moral accountability—that is, in treating people as passive products of the environment and victims of their own circumstances—we gradually erode any sense of personal responsibility. This means we have ushered in what one writer calls the "golden age of exoneration."[1] So it was that just outside of Washington, D.C., when police pulled over a car weaving from lane to lane and insisted the driver take a Breathalyzer test for intoxication, the woman (who turned out to be an orthopedic surgeon) became extraordinarily abusive, threatening what she would do to the officers if they ever ended up in her emergency room. When they handed her the Breathalyzer, she cursed and drop-kicked it across the road. The woman, who was by all accounts clearly drunk and clearly resisting arrest, was charged. But at her trial she raised the defense that she was not responsible for her behavior because she was experiencing premenstrual syndrome.[2] The judge acquitted her.

This is consistent with the notorious "Twinkie defense," named after the 1978 case in which a man pleaded temporary insanity after shooting a city supervisor in San Francisco's city hall. He insisted that a steady diet of junk food and sweets had raised his blood sugar and addled his brain: not the devil, but Twinkies made him do it.[3]

It has become virtually routine for defense lawyers to argue that defendants were abused as children, denied proper moral training, raised in abject poverty, plagued with learning disabilities, or something of the sort. The most brazen example of this excuse mentality was the much celebrated Menendez brothers case in California some years ago. Two young men, ages twenty-one and eighteen, shot and killed their parents in cold blood. At the trial their defense was that they had been sexually abused by their parents. They were acquitted (though later convicted on retrial). This may be the only literal enactment of the old joke about children who kill their parents and then plead for the mercy of the court because they are orphans.

But this mentality goes far beyond the criminal justice system. Mature, responsible adults, although amply warned that cigarettes can be dangerous to their health, nonetheless smoke, and when they get cancer, they sue the tobacco companies—successfully. Or take the case of the woman in Houston, Texas, who entered a hot-dog-eating contest in a nightclub. In her zeal to win, she ate too quickly and began to choke. Did she shrug off the natural consequence of her own absurd behavior? No, she decided she was a victim and sued the nightclub that sponsored the contest, arguing that the business was to blame because "the predictable result is that a contestant attempting to win the contest will choke on the hot dog."[4]

COARSENING OF CRIMES

This erosion of personal responsibility dulls the conscience and ultimately leads to the coarsening of crimes, as described in part 1. If you are constantly told that you are not responsible for your behavior, that you are simply a victim of circumstances, that society has left you out, does this not build a certain resentment toward those who are more successful? If you're not responsible, does this not justify your own baser instincts, releasing envy, covetousness, and anger that results in criminal acts?

I have walked through the cellblocks of more than six hundred prisons, coming face-to-face with young men and women who stare at me with vacant expressions. When I engage them in conversation, they will almost always (with the conspicuous exception of Christians) give me a long, sad, and angry story of how they have been unfairly treated in their lives; they feel their crime is simply the result of this ill treatment. Think about it: Why are we surprised by kids who kill without motive or reason but out of pent-up anger that they haven't had a fair deal from society or that they've been treated harshly by the criminal justice system? They feel they have an excuse for becoming embittered, violent, and dangerous, and the anger fuels increasingly coarse crimes.

DEHUMANIZATION OF THE INDIVIDUAL

When we think of justice in terms of either rehabilitative therapy or deterrence, the ultimate consequence is the dehumanization of the individual.

The therapeutic approach was brilliantly analyzed by C. S. Lewis in his essay "The Humanitarian Theory of Punishment." Lewis argued that theories of penology that aim to cure rather than to punish, though appearing to be mild and merciful, actually mean "that each one of us, from the moment he breaks the law, is deprived of the rights of a human being."[5] Those rights include being treated according to what one's conduct *deserves*. But the so-called humanitarian theory of punishment banishes all talk of just deserts, concerning itself only with the curing of antisocial conduct.

The humanitarian or therapeutic theory of punishment treats the wrongdoer as a laboratory animal rather than as a human being capable of moral choice. Furthermore, it takes decision making about penalties away from ordinary people and allocates them to a scientific elite. "To be 'cured' against one's will," wrote Lewis, "and cured of states which we may not regard as disease, is to be put on a level with those who have not yet reached the age of reason or those who never will; to be classed with infants, imbeciles, and domestic animals."[6]

Similarly the deterrent approach, which rests on the proposition that people can be frightened out of certain behavior, takes an equally low view of human nature. It is the favorite device of tyrants to manipulate people by fear.

I got a firsthand taste of this when I was in Bulgaria in 1996 to dedicate a hospital that Prison Fellowship had arranged to be constructed in the central prison, largely from surplus NATO equipment. The dedication service was attended by many ministers of the government and by the entire press corps of Sofia, the capital.

Bulgarian governmental officials at that time were still communists. In the first election after the fall of communism, officials simply ran under a new party label and were all elected; no one even changed offices. During the dedication service, I noticed that the minister of justice was almost visibly contemptuous of the proceedings, shifting back and forth in his place, ill at ease while Father Nikolai, the head of Prison Fellowship Bulgaria, was speaking and blessing the new facility.

When I spoke, I talked about the importance of the hospital for healing the body but the even greater importance of the prison chapel, which would cure the soul. Crime, I argued, was a moral problem. I noticed that the same minister of justice seemed riveted during my remarks. Afterward, he asked if I would meet him in his office.

The next morning, accompanied by Father Nikolai and my associates, I arrived at the office of the justice minister, who led us into a bare-walled conference room painted in characteristic communist drab green. He seated himself at the head of a long table, cigarette in hand, and immediately started firing questions in a brisk, business-like voice, speaking flawless English. "Mr. Colson, yesterday you said crime is a moral problem. Do you say that in a sociological sense?"

"No," I said. "Crime is a matter of people choosing to do wrong. It is the individual's moral failure."

He frowned, politely demurring, "It seems to me that crime is caused by social and economic forces, that people respond to environmental conditions."

It was my turn to demur. I argued that studies show that crime is caused by people making wrong moral choices.

But as our conversation continued, I could see how the minister's worldview affected his understanding of justice and why he couldn't understand me. Educated in a communist school system, he had been steeped in Marxist philosophy, which treats human beings as merely a complex form of matter. Their identity lies in the way they relate to other forms of matter—that is, what they produce and how they produce it. This is economic determinism. And the minister simply couldn't even grasp what I meant by individuals making moral choices.

This confusion was reflected in how he saw human beings and how order could be maintained in society. He set his cigarette pack on the table, using it to symbolize the barrier that the law sets up against certain behavior. Then his hand jumped over the pack to illustrate a criminal ignoring the law. "It seems that only fear will stop people from jumping over the law and committing crimes," he said, alluding to Talleyrand, the nineteenth-century French foreign minister who hung corpses in the street every night to deter the restless masses from fomenting revolution.

"No, sir," I responded. "Fear does not stop people. If it did, no one would smoke." The official juggled his cigarette pack nervously, and we both smiled.

The rest of the conversation was a fascinating lesson in how worldviews clash and how they lead us to totally different conclusions. But for our purposes here, what was vividly clear to me that day was what a low view the deterrent theory of crime really represents. Instead of seeing people as spiritual beings with dignity, he saw them merely as objects of society, objects that could be manipulated and kept under control by fear. This is the logical extension of the deterrent theory, and it is utterly dehumanizing.

But as C. S. Lewis saw so early and so clearly, the most insidious tyranny would arise from a therapeutic justice system. He wrote: "My contention is that good men (not bad men) consistently acting upon that position [humanitarian view] would act as cruelly and unjustly as the greatest tyrants. They might in some respects act even worse. Of all tyrannies, a tyranny sincerely exercised for the good of its victims may be the most oppressive. It may be better to live under robber barons than under omnipotent moral busybodies. The robber baron's cruelty may sometimes sleep, his cupidity may at some point be satiated; but those who torment us for our own good will torment us without end for they do so with the approval of their own conscience."[7]

One can see the frightening similarities between the humanitarian theory of punishment, as analyzed by Lewis, and the "soft tyranny" to which the great French statesman Alexis de Tocqueville saw democracies susceptible. Freedom-loving people, he predicted in the nineteenth century, would never submit to tyrannies of blood and iron, but they could quite easily allow government to assume more and more of the functions formerly left to private associations until finally it runs our lives for us—but "for our own good," of course, and with an unctuous bureaucratic smile.

COMPOUNDING OF EVIL

A fourth consequence of the utopian models of criminal justice is that we compound evil when we refuse to recognize it. The utopian framework of thought has taken away the conceptual tools that we need to grapple effectively with genuine evil. And when we cannot name or identify evil, we lose the capacity to deal with it. It then thrives with a vengeance.

I saw this a few years ago during a visit to Norway. The prisons there resemble the snow-draped landscape: cold and white. Norwegian prison officials are proud of their prison system, with its expensive, up-to-date facilities. They brag that, along with Sweden, they employ the most humane and progressive methods of treatment anywhere in the world, and many penologists agree.

The prison I visited just outside of Oslo was a model maximum-security facility. I was greeted by the warden, a psychiatrist with a clinically detached attitude. As she showed me through the sterile surroundings, which seemed more like a laboratory than a prison, she touted the number of counselors and the types of therapies given to inmates. In fact, we met so many other psychiatrists that I asked the warden how many of the inmates were mental cases.

"All of them, of course," she replied quickly, raising her eyebrows in surprise.

"What do you mean, 'all of them'?"

"Well, anyone who commits a violent crime is obviously mentally unbalanced."

Ah, yes. People are basically good, so anyone who could do something so terrible must be mentally ill. And the solution is therapy. I was seeing the therapeutic model fully realized. Tragically, I would also soon see its failure.

That day I spoke to an audience of inmates. Typically, prison is the one place where I don't have to belabor the message of sin; it's one biblical truth that men and women behind bars know well. But these inmates remained completely unmoved by anything I said, including the invitation to receive Christ. No response. Only glazed expressions.

As I was leaving, however, I was approached by an attractive young corrections officer who identified herself as a Christian. In perfect English she thanked me, then said, "I've prayed for this day, when these men would be confronted with a solid message of sin and salvation." She went on to describe her frustration at having to work within a flawed system in which there is no concept of personal responsibility and therefore no reason to seek personal transformation.

Only days later, her criticisms of the system were horribly borne out. By then, I had traveled on to Scotland, where I received an urgent phone call from the Norwegian Prison Fellowship workers. They soberly informed me that the Christian officer I had met had been assigned to escort an inmate out to see a movie, an R-rated movie at that; it was considered part of the inmate's therapy. On the way back, he had overpowered her, raped her, and then murdered her.

A sign of mental illness? A result of social or economic forces? How pale and ineffective such explanations appear beside the monstrosity of human cruelty and violence. When we embrace nonmoral categories to explain away moral evil, we fail to take it seriously, and we fail to constrain it. When we refuse to listen to the true diagnosis of the sickness of the soul, we will not find a true remedy, and in the end our blindness will destroy us.

A REALISTIC VIEW OF
HUMAN NATURE

WHAT WE HAVE seen is that a wrong worldview about human nature has been the root problem in our criminal justice system throughout the twentieth century. It is responsible for a system that has failed to halt crime, in the process has created the prison leviathan, and even more seriously has been responsible for an attitude that can only lead to a loss of moral responsibility, a further coarsening of crime, a dehumanization of the individual, and a compounding of evil.

What lesson do we draw from this? The chaos that results from such failure poses a grave danger, for in any society only two forces hold the sinful nature in check: the restraint of conscience or the restraint of the sword. The less that citizens have of the former, the more the state must employ the latter. A society that fails to keep order by an appeal to civic duty and moral responsibility (and especially a society that fails to maintain a sound justice system) must resort to more and more coercion. It will be either open coercion, as practiced by totalitarian states, or covert coercion, the kind C. S. Lewis described, where people are wooed into believing that what is being done to them is for their own benefit.

And the tragedy—and real danger of our flawed anthropology—is that people will readily accept a sacrifice of liberty to achieve order. It is a Faustian bargain that people have always made, most vividly illustrated by the Germans in the 1930s, but in many other contexts as well.

We have already seen the danger when crime so threatens the order that the public is faced with the choice between liberty and order. At the height of the crime wave in the early 1990s, when people were afraid to walk in the streets at night, many communities imposed curfews ordering people to stay off the streets after a prescribed hour. Curfews were immensely popular even though they are, of course, a form of martial law. At one point, thousands of communities in America had instituted them.[1]

A 1993 poll taken in the Miami, Florida, area found that 76 percent of the respondents favored curfews for people under age eighteen and that 71 percent favored random roadblocks to search for weapons, even though that would be a clear violation of our constitutional protections.[2]

Around the same time the governor of Puerto Rico called out the military National Guard to preserve order in the streets. Vacationers at expensive hotels along the beaches of San Juan saw troops with camouflage uniforms and M16s patrolling among kids bouncing beach balls back and forth.[3] Various jurisdictions formed special police units.

The mayor of Washington, D.C., at that time proposed calling out the National Guard to patrol the streets of our nation's capital.

People in Britain have witnessed the same phenomenon. In 1994 the Major government proposed a dramatic reshaping of the British criminal justice system, curtailing traditional rights, increasing police powers, and imposing stricter penalties for a broad variety of major and minor offenses. The prime minister was bitterly attacked by the opposition party, with some justification in my opinion, for setting aside concepts that originated centuries ago in the English common law and were the inspiration for provisions contained in our Bill of Rights in the United States. The laws that followed allowed governmental officials to bug phones or order break-ins to homes, and the police gained the right to hold people for seven days without a warrant. Legislation also provided incarceration of juvenile offenders down to the age of twelve and gave health departments the authority to compile registers of mentally ill individuals who might perpetrate violence. Michael Howard, then home secretary, even proposed a national DNA bank to help track down criminals.[4] Even the generally conservative magazine *The Economist* was sharply critical, though it acknowledged that the government was acting to satisfy rising public fear over crime.[5]

Fortunately, perhaps even providentially, crime began to decline at the very moment when the public outcry for order posed a genuine threat to the constitutional tradition that so zealously guards civil liberties. But the lesson should not be lost on us: If people feel that order is threatened, and if government cannot maintain its first responsibility, then people will gladly surrender their liberties to achieve peace and security. Alexis de Tocqueville may have been too optimistic: even freedom-loving societies may embrace hard tyranny, as well as the soft kind, when the perceived alternative is disorder.

All of this underscores how vitally important it is that a criminal justice system fulfills its prescribed function to preserve order in a legitimate way. To meet the test of justice, a criminal justice system must start by taking a realistic view of human nature—taking into account the inherent propensity toward sin and evil—and must proceed to treat offenders as morally responsible beings. Original sin means that human nature is flawed, but it does not mean we are without hope. Individual acts of sin are neither compelled by our nature nor free from moral responsibility.

Terrible consequences have come from Western society's long flirtations with bad anthropology: It has led to huge increases both in rates of crime and in growth of the state. Restoration of justice is impossible without restoration of good anthropology.

The good news is that once we take a realistic view of human nature, we find immediately the key to the cause of crime. It is not environment or poverty but wrong moral choices. The truth is, we are not deprived, we are depraved. And the biblical worldview not only offers us realism about who we are but also hope about what we can be, both as individuals and as a culture. There is a way out— one that is neither utopian nor manipulative.

PART THREE

REDEMPTION

THE MORAL ROOTS OF CRIME

WHEN I WAS selected to receive the Templeton Prize in 1993, I was invited to receive the medal and accompanying check at Buckingham Palace. The presentation would be made by His Royal Highness the Duke of Edinburgh. Of course these events have fairly rigid protocols. I was told that upon being introduced to Prince Philip, I should respond briefly to any remarks he might make to me, but under no circumstances was I to prolong my reply or, heaven forbid, initiate conversation with him. I was also warned that these ceremonies were to be brief: the award handed over, a two-minute response, and that would be it.

When we arrived at Buckingham Palace at the appointed hour,

I was escorted into one of the grand reception rooms, followed by the judges of the Templeton Prize, members of the House of Lords, and other dignitaries. We were gathered in a long line to await Prince Philip's arrival. The mood was appropriately solemn.

After I received the medal and the check from Prince Philip, I gave a succinct two-minute response, as instructed. Prince Philip then said that perhaps I could help him understand why there was so much crime among young people. As it happened, some alarming statistics had just been released in Britain.

Aware of the mandate to be brief, I suggested that the problem would best be solved by sending more young Brits to Sunday school. There was a ripple of chuckles through the crowd, and Prince Philip smiled, assuming that I was attempting some humor.

"No, no," I assured him. I then proceeded into a rather lengthy explanation of how religious instruction correlates positively with lower crime rates across all nationalities, classes, and races.

In fact, I shared with the prince and others some British crime statistics that I had learned from Christie Davies, of the University of Reading. For example, during the dramatic rise of youth crime in the past half century, attendance at Sunday school declined, from 46 percent of the under-fifteen population in 1931, to 20 percent in 1961, to just 14 percent in 1989. Conversely, Sunday school attendance soared during the nineteenth century, from a mere 12 percent of youth under age fifteen in 1818, to 38 percent in 1851, to 52 percent in 1891, and to a peak of 53 percent in 1901.[1] And that rise during the late nineteenth century coincided—if coincidence it be—with a decline in crime.

This conversation may not have been good protocol, strictly speaking, but Prince Philip seemed enthralled. Perhaps the reason this conversation took on a certain life of its own was that the underlying point was so obvious yet so rarely articulated: Criminal acts are moral choices. If you want to reduce youth crime, you will have to restock the moral resource kit that young people take into the world. For the time being, that kit stands drastically depleted by the relativism, subjectivism, and other Enlightenment heirlooms that we discussed in part 1.

WE HAVE MET THE ENEMY

As discussed in part 2, theories of crime have come and gone over the past three hundred years. Experts have urged that crime is caused by poverty; yet we know that historically crime has actually increased in times of general prosperity and decreased in times of general want. Other experts have claimed that crime is caused by race or racism; yet it has proven impossible to correlate race to crime. In various studies among children from the same racial and economic circumstances, researchers have been baffled by the question of why some children do not commit crimes and others do. Still other experts—including those involved in the conservative "law and order" movement of the late 1960s, and I was part of that group—thought crime was the result of the rational calculation of probable gains versus probable losses. Yet we now know not only that decision making is much more complex than that but also that decision making is a moral enterprise, which will inevitably be conducted in an amoral manner when decision makers grow up in an amoral environment.

So what is the cause of crime? It turns out the Bible was right all along. *Humans are responsible for sin and evil.* In contrast to the ritual cleanliness of the Pharisees, who saw individuals as capable of being defiled by unclean foods going into them, Jesus stressed that defilement comes from the heart—that is, from the seat of the will. Consider Mark 7:20-23: "What comes out of a man is what makes him 'unclean.' For from within, out of men's hearts, come evil thoughts, sexual immorality, theft, murder, adultery, greed, malice, deceit, lewdness, envy, slander, arrogance and folly. All these evils come from inside and make a man 'unclean.' "

In the epistle to the Romans, Paul stressed that sinfulness is part of our predicament as human beings, regardless of our bloodline. "Jews and Gentiles alike are all under sin," he declares in Romans 3:9, backing up his statement with an Old Testament quotation, "There is no one righteous, not even one" (Romans 3:10). And in Romans 7:15, he exclaims on behalf of all humanity: "I don't understand myself at all, for I really want to do what is right, but I don't do it. Instead, I do the very thing I hate" (NLT).

In his *Confessions* Saint Augustine highlights the same truth about human behavior in the famous passage about stealing a pear. He wrote: "I willed to commit theft, not because I was driven to it by any need. . . . For I stole a thing of which I had plenty of my own and of much better quality. Nor did I wish to enjoy that thing which I desired to gain by theft, but rather to enjoy the actual theft and the sin of the theft. . . . Foul was the evil, and I loved it."[2]

Since Augustine elsewhere in the *Confessions* accuses himself of worse sins than stealing pears, some have wondered why he stops to discuss this one particular crime. I think he did it to showcase the irreducible element of human choice in evil acts. He may have been influenced by the desirability of the pears or by social factors, such as wanting to impress the buddies he was with at the time, but none of these factors—or all of them combined—overrode his will. To steal the pears, he had to make an affirmative decision to do something he knew was wrong.

The Christian approach to human responsibility for human acts precludes any excuses based on heredity, upbringing, economics, or anything else. These things can influence us, but ultimately we are responsible for our acts. This is the Christian view, and I think Judaism and Islam stand with Christians on this issue. All three agree with the great American comic-strip character Pogo, who said, "We have met the enemy, and he is us."

The empirical evidence of recent decades completely affirms Pogo, or, more properly said, it affirms the biblical view of human nature and its relationship to crime. Two studies in particular seem to offer indisputable evidence.

The first was the landmark work of psychologist Stanton Samenow and the late psychiatrist Samuel Yochelson. Back in the 1960s these researchers believed, as most people did, that crime was caused by the criminal's environment. To test this hypothesis, they did a study that stretched over seventeen years. It involved in-depth examinations of the lives of two hundred fifty inmates in Washington, D.C., with thousands of hours of clinical testing. Their work was published in 1982 under the title *The Criminal Personality*. By that time, Samenow and Yochelson had changed their minds. No longer did they believe that environment, poverty, or oppression was the origin of crime. Crime, they concluded, in every case, was "the product of deliberation"; it was the result of individuals making wrong moral choices. The answer to criminal behavior, in their view, therefore, was the "conversion to a whole new [responsible] lifestyle."[3]

The second study, a landmark work entitled *Crime and Human Nature,* was published in 1986 by Harvard professors James Q. Wilson and Richard Herrnstein. They found virtually no correlation between crime and the usual suspects such as race, poverty, or oppression. But they did find a strong correlation between crime and moral training. They ended up concluding that, while other factors may influence people's moral decisions, there is no escaping the fact that crime essentially involves decision making on moral issues: "Conscience and justice (or equity) are not philosophical abstractions that clutter up the straightforward business of finding a scientific explanation for criminality; they are a necessary part of the explanation itself, and as such they (along with an individual's time horizon and sensitivity to the reinforcements associated with a course of action) can help us understand criminal behavior and the social structures that deal with it."[4]

(I must acknowledge that they also found a possible genetic component: Children of parents in jail were far more likely than others to end up in jail themselves. I am not a genetic determinist. I suggest what we have here is not an independent cause of crime but a further example of Wilson's and Herrnstein's primary culprit: a lack of moral training. After all, parents in prison are in no position to give moral training to their children, and it is unlikely that any substitute for the parents will do so either. This is one reason why we must redouble our efforts to reach the children of prisoners. It is also why I am so concerned about the high—and growing—number of mothers currently incarcerated for petty drug, theft, and fraud offenses. One of the unintended consequences of "mandatory minimum sentencing" schemes has unnecessarily created a whole generation of orphans. But that's a subject for a later chapter.)

What Samenow and Yochelson as well as Wilson and Herrnstein discovered in their studies is precisely what I have seen in my own relationships with inmates. Criminals generally will find some way to blame either the criminal justice system, their deprived backgrounds, race, or other factors for their own plight of being in prison. In prison for seven months, I heard endless laments about the unfairness of the criminal justice system. But as I got to know the person better, as I probed and asked questions, it became very clear that the person knew precisely what he was doing. When I got past all the protective armor, I discovered that the person got into drugs because it was profitable, even though he knew that it was wrong. Members of organized crime told me that it was a way of life—their friends and neighbors all did it—but they still knew that it was the wrong thing for them.

The law is indeed written on our hearts (see Psalm 40:8). Some people are moved by the thrill of crime, but even then they know they have done wrong. I have never met an inmate who told me that he stole prescription drugs to take care of his sick wife because public health facilities would not make available what she needed. This is one of the classic dilemmas posed in college ethics courses, but I have never encountered it or anything close to it in real life in decades of talking to convicts.

Of all the inmates I've met, the Christians are the quickest to acknowledge their own moral failure and to dispense with the typical excuses. One former decorated New York police officer told me that he had gone to the police force with high ideals. But making drug busts night after night, he saw mounds of evidence worth hundreds of thousands of dollars on the street. As he put it to me, the temptation simply became overpowering. He knew full well what he was doing when he pocketed some of those drugs and later sold them. He was eventually caught in a sting operation and sent to prison.

So we have crime because human beings make wrong moral choices, and human beings make wrong moral choices because their natures are distorted by the primal error that goes by the name of *original sin,* as discussed in part 2. Yet many people seem willfully blind to this insight, perhaps because it seems so harsh, or more likely because it is so personally convicting.

This blindness can manifest itself in unexpected ways. Recently a friend told me about philosopher Mortimer Adler's experience in giving a talk at a Reform Jewish synagogue in Washington, D.C. A few years ago Adler converted from Judaism to Christianity, so there was potential for some coldness between him and his audience. As my friend told it, there was indeed some chilliness—but not on the basis of Adler's conversion. Instead, it set in at the point when Adler said that the three great monotheistic religions—Judaism, Christianity, and Islam—represent the only reasonable choices for mankind and that we must choose on the basis of reason and truth. The audience did not object to any defense of Christianity against Judaism because Adler was not offering any such defense on this occasion. All he had done was assert the superiority of the three great monotheistic religions—which hold individuals personally accountable to God—against all other religious options. That was all it took to alienate this audience of people supposedly committed to one of those three religions.

THE MORAL ROOTS OF CULTURE

But moral choices, it should be noted, are never made in a vacuum. While the law is written on the human heart, as the Bible tells us, the conscience must be trained. It is informed by a variety of institutions, beginning most prominently with the family but including almost every aspect of culture. Most important, conscience is informed by religious truth. So as we consider the cause of crime, we need to look at the moral roots of culture.

Conservatives have always rebelled against the notion of looking for root causes for crime because the idea of root causes was for so long used by liberals. As we discussed in chapter 5, the Ramsey Clark ideology asserted that "root causes" of crime are poverty and injustice and that we could cure crime by transferring resources away from law enforcement into educational and social programs that will make these ills disappear.

The Cultural Power of Religion

But just because the liberals picked the wrong root causes does not mean there aren't root causes. There are, and they are moral in nature. They are the deterioration of a society's moral fabric, that moral ethos that makes it impossible to form a consensus by which the conscience can be shaped.

For example, we see the relationship between culture and crime dramatically illustrated in the study that I referred to in my unexpected conversation with the Duke of Edinburgh. Christie Davies breaks the recent social history of Britain into three periods.

The first period, from 1860 to 1905, saw *rising* religious adherence and church membership, *falling* crimes of violence and dishonesty, and *falling* illegitimacy. Drug and alcohol abuse also *fell,* albeit less evenly.

The second period, from 1905 to 1960, saw religious adherence and church membership *falling* slowly and unevenly, crimes of violence and dishonesty *rising* slowly and unevenly, illegitimacy remaining *low* (except during wartime), and drug and alcohol abuse *falling.* The bad economy of the early 1930s did not in itself cause any upward spike in crime.

The third period, from 1960 to the present, shows religious adherence and church membership *falling* rapidly, crimes of violence and dishonesty *rising* rapidly, illegitimacy also *rising* rapidly, and drug and alcohol abuse *rising* as well.[5]

So, contrary to modern conventional wisdom, culture and the cultural power of religion clearly have more influence on criminal behavior than economic factors do.

James Q. Wilson, the great American criminologist, made a similar discovery. He found that during the rapid urbanization of the United States during the mid-nineteenth century, when one might expect crime rates to rise, they actually fell. And what else was taking place besides urbanization? A great spiritual awakening, as it happens. As Wilson explains, morality took hold neck and neck with industrialization. Conversely, during the 1920s—a time of such economic plenty that you would think there would be no incentive for crime—crime, in fact, increased. Why? Because, as Wilson and Herrnstein wrote, the educated classes began to repudiate moral uplift, and Freud's psychological theories came into vogue.[6] The dominant ethos shifted from viewing human beings as inclined toward sin and needing moral formation, to viewing them as having wonderful "naturally good" selves that need only "liberation" to flower, just as Rousseau had said they would.

Then came the Great Depression. With all that unemployment and poverty and deprivation, one would think crime would go up. But like Davies, Wilson and Herrnstein found that crime actually fell. Tough times develop strength of character; they also cause human networks such as extended families and benevolent associations to pull together, creating more of what Michael Schluter and David Lee in their book *The R Factor* call "encounter relationships," face-to-face relationships in which people are willingly accountable to one another and help one another out.[7] A society that is rich in these types of relationships, as will be argued more fully later, will have low crime rates. Times of dizzying prosperity, on the other hand, leave people free to seek self-satisfaction and to be moral loners.[8]

Surely one of the most dramatic examples of the power of religion to influence behavior and particularly discourage crime occurred in Wales in the Great Revival of 1904. It started with the preaching of Evan Roberts and soon spread from church to church. The great historian J. Edwin Orr reports that the revival had such an effect on Wales that, after the 1905 New Year, the Swansea County Police Court announced there had not been a single charge for drunkenness on the holiday weekend, the first time ever. At the new year, there were 40 percent fewer people in jail in Cardiff. As Orr puts it, a "great wave of sobriety which swept over the country . . . closed many of the taverns. Stocks of Bibles were sold out. [It even affected work, but in a surprising way.] So many men had given up foul language that the pit ponies dragging the coal trucks in the mine tunnels did not understand what was being said to them. Gamblers were converted, stolen goods were returned, court calendars cleared, and police complained they had nothing to do."[9]

Michael Novak, a leading Catholic theologian and economist, offered some interesting insights into the relationship between moral climate and crime when he spoke to a Justice Fellowship conference in Washington in 1994. The United States, Novak argued, started out with a disorder problem: Having thrown off the authority of Britain, some Americans thought all authority had been thrown off, and petty crime and public drunkenness became very common from the 1780s to the 1830s. What, then, caused this problem to turn around in 1830? As Novak pointed out, several things coalesced around 1830: the Sunday school movement, the temperance movement, and a spiritual revival called the Second Great Awakening. So Novak, like Wilson, argued that one sees in this trend the primacy of cultural factors, especially religious ones.

What Causes Virtue?

But Novak had an even more important point to make, which leads us to the more important question of what we are to do about crime in the light of this. In economics, most policy experts have by now gotten past the mistake of asking what causes poverty. As Novak quipped: What have you got if you answer the question, What causes poverty? Only a way to create more poverty! The point is that there was an erroneous assumption behind the question; it assumed that wealth was the normal human condition, with poverty being the exception that calls for an explanation—which is absurd. Today economic policy makers spend much more time answering the question, What causes wealth? The architects of this change of stance can point to many excellent results.

In criminal justice, Novak pointed out, we need to make a similar adjustment. We used to ask—and to some extent we still do ask—What causes crime? This question has the same problem as the question, What causes poverty? If we knew for certain what causes crime, we would know how to cause *more* crime, but we wouldn't necessarily know how to cause *less*. What causes crime? is the wrong question. Just as the question, What causes poverty? assumed that wealth was the natural human state, the question What causes crime? assumes that virtuous conduct is the natural human course of action. After Eden, that's not the case, despite the great myth perpetrated by modern utopians. The questions we should be asking therefore are questions such as, Why did the person I just passed *not* pick my pocket? Why did the person ahead of me in line at the bank *not* rob the place?

Granted, most people you pass on the street will not steal your money, and you will not usually find yourself standing behind a bank robber while waiting to make a deposit. But this is not because people are naturally good; it is because there are still some schools of virtue that are up and running. The transmission of standards of decent conduct, though breaking down, has not yet ground to a halt.

As Novak pointed out, the key question is not, What causes crime?; it is, What causes virtue? And Novak's answer, briefly, is clearly not economic; rather, it is the cultivation of virtue, not only virtuous behavior in individuals but the encouragement of cultures that teach and expect virtue.[10] This means, in Novak's view, reinvigorating those small intermediate structures of society such as families, churches, and community groups.

So this brings us to the critical question perhaps of this entire book: What can be done to bring about virtue in individuals as they make moral choices?

THE MORAL ANSWER

WHAT CAN BE done to produce virtuous cultures?

The answer is two words: *moral reformation*. I once sat in a class at the InnerChange Freedom Initiative, the full-time Christian prison program Prison Fellowship U.S.A. runs in Houston, Texas. I listened to a lecture by a tall, articulate African-American inmate. He asked the group: "Does anyone know what's wrong with therapy? I know all about therapy programs because I've been in prison six times and have taken therapy sessions every time. I'll tell you what's wrong with therapy: I'm still in prison."

He went on to explain that the problem with therapy is that it merely teaches one how to manage one's sin. The right solution, he said, is transformation, that is, finding a way to get out of one's sin.

Getting out of it. Getting out of sin. That's what this is all about. The solution to crime is no different from—indeed, it is a subset of—the solution to the human predicament as a whole. We are at odds with God; we cannot repair this situation ourselves; God has repaired it for us and offers us a part of that great eternal solution.

The question for us at this point is, How can individuals, and also societies, be transformed? I have given away the answer by saying that the solution is a Christian one. But to support that claim, I should first examine other alternatives. Do worldviews other than the Christian one offer a way out of our predicament? Do they offer *redemption?*

DO OTHER RELIGIONS OFFER REDEMPTION?

Today there is a resurgence of interest in Islam, particularly in prisons. To many, especially to people of non-Western background, it offers a monotheistic option that is bold, brash, and self-confident. But the problem is that Islam has never been about redemption because it does not believe God can or ever would enter into a personal relationship with any of his creatures. The Islamic God is lord and master, like the Judeo-Christian God, but unlike the Judeo-Christian God, Allah is not *father.* Pious Muslims moreover consider blasphemous the idea that God would so debase himself as to become a human, suffer torture and death, rise with a real body, and invite his creatures into a personal relationship with him. And Muslims have a very grim prospect when it comes to the question of salvation because for the Muslim heaven is achieved only after a perilous walk across the sword of judgment.

Then there is the very delicate issue of the Jews, among whom I have many dear friends. The Jews, having decided that the preacher from Nazareth who appeared in their midst one generation before the fall of the temple was not the Messiah, recommitted themselves to trying to live by the Law. In the great scholarly ventures of the Talmud and the Mishnah, they investigated the depths and technicalities of the Law, the better to live it. Yet the task remains as impossible today as Peter found it to be when he warned Jewish Christians against it in Acts 15:10. The Law does not provide the transformation we are looking for, not only because it is impossible to observe, but also because observing it does not bring transformation. It was never meant to. It was meant to purify and sanctify God's people during the long period of waiting for the Messiah. That is why God in the Old Testament commands that sacrifices be offered in the temple, yet Scripture also says that he desires mercy and justice and not empty sacrifices (Hosea 6:6; see Isaiah 1). The Law was a placeholder—a holy one, a divinely ordained one, but a placeholder nonetheless. It was not, and is not, the way to redemption. I say this with all respect for the Jewish people and with all awareness that the decision of who is and is not saved is ultimately God's.

I am speaking, of course, of Orthodox Judaism; other Jews have dealt with the dilemma of the Law by taking on board the essential principles of the Enlightenment, thus relativizing the Law and allowing ways of life that are indistinguishable from those of the secularist majority. This solution has allowed many Jews to reach heights of leadership in secular affairs and to contribute greatly to human culture, but it does not offer the transformation, the redemption, that we are seeking.

Does Hinduism offer a solution? C. S. Lewis for a time thought it offered the only credible alternative to Christianity, yet he found it wanting, perhaps because its endless cycles of reincarnation afford no true redemption. In fact, of all the places I have preached in the world, I have found the Hindu culture to be afflicted with the greatest sense of hopelessness and in turn the greatest hunger to hear the Good News.

A number of years ago I visited the major prison in the province of Kerala, India. It was an old British colonial institution with high red-brick walls and huge, imposing gates in front. I was met by the prison governor, the local officials, and khaki-clad Indian guards, who marched us from the entrance to the center podium. One could almost hear the "Colonel Bogey March" being played in the background.

I stood on the platform and stared out at a thousand inmates clad only in white loincloths, crouched down, most of them with their eyes cast downward as if to avoid eye contact. These were truly outcasts, untouchables, and their downcast expressions reflected their sense of shame and lowliness.

As I spoke that day, I talked about Jesus, who went to the cross to pay the penalty for our sins; how he, a prisoner, died for us so that we could be forgiven and free and have a new life in him. I watched the inmates' eyes widen, expressions turn from despair to hope. The more I talked about Jesus' taking our sins on himself, the more emotion filled the faces of these men. I could only imagine what was going through their minds. They had committed a crime in a totally unforgiving culture. They had been cast away in an unspeakably grim dungeon. They had no hope, for when they returned to the streets, they would still be outcasts. And as Hindus they thought that the evil they had done to someone else in this life would be done to them in the next life—an endless cycle that perpetuates suffering and evil, the very opposite of salvation. If what I was saying to them was true, then Jesus was offering them forgiveness, redemption, hope, and transformation.

When I led the inmates in prayer that day, I senses that many people were committing themselves to Christ. I sensed it from the holy hush in the crowd. I sensed it from the look on their faces. I sensed it from their bowed heads. All through the crowd I saw men raising their hands.

Following the prayer, they looked up, and many eyes were filled with tears. I did something completely impulsive; I wanted more than anything else for these untouchables to know that I would touch them. So I jumped off the platform, looking at the startled expressions on the guards and officials, and walked straight into the midst of the ranks of the thousand men crouched before me in the mud. All at once, as with a flight of birds, they rose up and surrounded me, and for the next twenty minutes, I did nothing but reach out to respond to their touches as they took turns coming up to put their hands on me.

Why did they do this? Not because I was a celebrity; they had never heard of Chuck Colson or Watergate (probably had never heard of Richard Nixon). They were desperate to "touch," to know that the love God offers is real. No, Hinduism falls sadly short; it cannot provide salvation.

Buddhism speaks of something called nirvana, which post-Christian Westerners have long seen as similar to the Christian concept of salvation. As G. K. Chesterton once observed: People are always saying that Buddhism and Christianity are very much alike—especially Buddhists. But nirvana is a world-denying state. At best, it offers a path of transient individual mysticism. It offers no true transformation of individuals or societies.

Then there is the New Age option, which is essentially a blend of Eastern religious themes, watered down and sweetened for consumption by narcissistic Westerners. Essentially, the points I have made about Hinduism and Buddhism are equally valid against the New Age option, with one difference, very much to the disadvantage of the New Age. The major Eastern religions at least teach genuine disciplines. They demand something from their followers. It takes effort to become a mystic in these religions. In the New Age, by contrast, one of the dominant themes is effortlessness. It's perfectly tailored for Western consumerists, who want some "spirituality" and who want it fast. It's a religion for the microwave era. At its best and taking its claims at face value, it offers personal tranquillity, success, and getting in touch with the "universal spirit of which we are all a part." But it does not even *claim* to offer the kind of redemption humans seek.

People look for transformation in yet other ways. Many people once thought—and some still do—that if we got rid of traditional sexual morality, we could usher in a new world of carefree fun for all. Others thought drugs would do the trick. (Remember Aldous Huxley's *The Doors of Perception* or his *Brave New World*?)

The twentieth century also saw a host of liberation philosophies and theologies, most inspired by Karl Marx. We were told that if only we could be free from the oppressive structures of society and the powerful classes, we could find our salvation and deliverance. Science once promised its own form of liberation: knowledge would give us the progress that would deliver us from our oppressed states. Even today we see commercials appealing to the deepest human desire and offering materialistic salvation. The Volvo ad is one current example; it shows a person standing under a waterfall. As the handsome figure looks skyward, a soothing theatrical voice says, "Volvo can save your soul."[1]

THE GOSPEL OF CHRIST

We need only look at any area of life today to hear secular promises of redemption. So deeply ingrained in the human soul is the need for salvation, an answer to the dilemmas of life, that advertisers, philosophers, teachers, and others across the board attempt to address this deepest of all human needs. But the truth is that only Christianity deals directly with what individuals most long for: true redemption, true forgiveness of sin.

The gospel addresses the human dilemma directly. First, it recognizes the source of the suffering and sin that plague us: Sin is in us; we are responsible. But God so loves us that he came in the flesh to pay the price for our sins (see John 3:16). When Jesus, the Son of God, was crucified on the cross, he took on himself the sins of mankind. This was the great sacrifice, a one-time-for-all atonement for the sins of humanity. God's demands for justice were met by Christ; justice and mercy met at the cross, and by our faith, which is a gracious gift of God, we are then declared righteous. God's righteousness, by virtue of Christ's sacrifice on our behalf, is imputed to us; his righteousness is credited to us. We are thus saved from our sins not by our efforts but by God's grace alone (see Ephesians 2:4-5, 8-9). We are redeemed, and this is the greatest news ever.

Once people experience this redemption, they are so filled with gratitude to the God who made it possible that they then genuinely desire to live a new and different life—one in obedience to the One who saved them. This is what has driven me to take the gospel back into the prisons for one reason and one reason alone: I know God has called me to it, and out of gratitude for what he did twenty-six years ago in saving me, forgiving my sins, and giving me a new life, I have no alternative but to respond to his call.

This is the very essence of transformation. Not only is the heart transformed and the head transformed—not only do we feel and understand the need to be different, to be new in Christ—but we are given the *will* to do what God commands, to seek to be righteous. This is the argument that C. S. Lewis makes so brilliantly in "Men without Chests." The "head," he argues, may know what is right, but the appetites of the "stomach" cannot be controlled by reason. He contends that only when the "spirited element" (in his analogy, the "chest" or the will) is strengthened can it rein in the passions and appetite of the stomach. Lewis's point, of course, is that in today's culture we make "men without chests," and as he puts it with exquisite irony, "we expect of them virtue and enterprise." And "we castrate and bid the geldings be fruitful."[2]

As Lewis argues so eloquently, the will becomes the indispensable ingredient in personal transformation. Only when the will is converted do we have the capacity to *do* what is right and just; only the transformation of the will can deal with the problem of crime at its roots.

I surely discovered this to be so in my life. I was raised in a good family. I always looked forward to Sunday afternoons when I would have time with my father, who was otherwise studying at school at night and working long hours to keep our family fed. On those Sunday afternoons he would lecture me in what I now recognize to be the Puritan ethic. "Always tell the truth," he told me, "and you'll never be in trouble. Work hard. Earn your living. Be industrious. Never cheat or take something that doesn't belong to you." I had about as good an ethical training as any child could hope for.

In college I studied political philosophy. I learned about Kant's categorical imperative and was familiar with most of the ethical formulations of the great philosophers.

When I went to the White House to be President Nixon's counsel, I took all the prudent steps to avoid conflicts, including divesting myself completely of my interest in what was then a very successful law firm. I placed all of my assets in a blind trust in a major bank. I refused to see anyone who had been a previous client. I had nothing to do with any matters that I had handled while practicing as a lawyer. I even refused to accept gifts at Christmas, turning them over instead to the telephone operators in the White House or to the driver of my limousine. No one would corrupt me—or so I thought.

Yet I went to prison.

How could that be? The answer is that the human heart is, as

Scripture tells us, deceitful (see Jeremiah 17:9). And human beings have an infinite capacity for self-rationalization.

The problem, I now realize, is that I had convinced myself that I would do no wrong, yet I slowly and gradually succumbed to peer pressure, and my will was not strong enough to resist. We are never more dangerous than when we are self-righteous.

But is this merely religious theory, or does Christianity truly transform a person? Admittedly, even with a transformed will, Christians can continue to justify themselves, succumb to peer pressures, and fall. But the evidence is overwhelming that when the will is converted, the general result is transformed behavior.

I have repeatedly seen the evidence in prisons. As mentioned earlier, Prison Fellowship U.S.A. runs a prison known as the InnerChange Freedom Initiative, the first Christian prison in America, modeled after two that operated for many years in South America, known there as the APAC program. The APAC prisons in South America have reported over many years a recidivism rate of less than 5 percent. Although we've been operating the prison in Texas for only two and one-half years, we have begun to have some evidence of its success. Of those inmates who have completed the entire eighteen-month prescribed program, which emphasizes transformation and not therapy, only one has reoffended. Of the total of more than one hundred who have been released, so far only eight have been rearrested for new offenses. (As encouraging as that figure is, it is still misleading because it includes some people who were in the program for only a matter of weeks or perhaps a couple of months, not long enough really to be measured.)

A more representative study, perhaps, was published by researchers of the National Institute for Healthcare Research in 1997.[3] Using data on New York prisoners who attended Prison Fellowship programs, the researchers looked at recidivism rates for those prisoners as compared with a matched control group. The recidivism rate for the control group was 41 percent. But the recidivism rate for those who attended ten or more Prison Fellowship Bible studies was cut to 14 percent, a dramatic two-thirds reduction!

But let me put a personal face on individual transformation and the power of the gospel to create a new life. Over nearly a quarter century of ministry, I have received no greater reward than seeing lives transformed. I have seen men and women broken in the pit of prison, their families shattered, their hope gone, then transformed by Christ, given a new life, and often restored to their families. Wherever I go today, at almost any meeting, someone will come to me and say, "I was in prison, and my life was in shambles. I'm now out, working, and my life is back together. Thank God for your ministry." I am frequently driven to my knees in gratitude to God for these evidences of his grace. I call these men and women our "living monuments."

Let me tell you about just a few. Several years ago, I was invited to a gathering of several hundred ex-convicts, a regional gathering of what we call the Network for Life, a postprison support group much like Alcoholics Anonymous, in which ex-offenders help one another. When I walked into the room to the jubilant gathering, one man in particular elbowed through the crowd, came over, and threw his arms around me. Leon, a six-foot-six African-American, looked down at me and said, "You kept your word." Suddenly I remembered.

I had first met Leon in 1981, when I was touring a housing project in a ghetto area of Los Angeles. Leon, an ex-offender, was working with a group of inmates. He had a stern and forbidding expression. When he met me that first time, he grabbed my hand, pulled me close, and said, "Colson, don't mess up."

I looked at him, a bit startled, and said, "I won't."

He repeated it, "Colson, don't mess up. There are a lot of guys in prison depending on you. You mess up, and you'll let them down."

A second time I assured him I would not.

The third time he was more emphatic: "Colson, don't mess up. You do, and I'll kill you."

That got my attention.

It was the same Leon now embracing me, rejoicing at what God had done in his life and mine over these many years.

Then there was Danny Croce. Danny had been a construction worker in the suburbs of Boston, Massachusetts, a poor kid who grew up on the streets, making his way by fistfighting, semiprofessionally, in fact. But Danny also spent most of his evenings in barrooms and hanging around with a gang. As he told me, he never expected to live to adulthood.

Late one night, after spending the whole evening in a bar, Danny drove home in a blinding rain. Suddenly a figure arose before him. He heard a thud, and when he got out of the car, he discovered that he had hit and killed a police officer.

Danny found himself in a prison cell, utterly dejected and in such despair he might have ended his life. Another inmate gave Danny a Bible, however, and for the first time in his life Danny read about Jesus. A few days later he asked to see the chaplain, who explained the gospel to him, and that very night Danny knelt by his bunk and surrendered his life to Christ.

Gradually, old habits changed, and Danny Croce discovered himself, though still in prison, a free man. During his time in prison, he was, as he put it, "blown away" that Prison Fellowship volunteers cared for his family and took presents to his kids at Christmastime through our Angel Tree program. Upon his release, Danny went to work in Boston, helping disadvantaged kids. Someone told him about a Charles W. Colson Scholarship at Wheaton College in Illinois, available only for ex-offenders. Danny applied, was accepted, and a few years ago graduated with a degree in Bible and theology. He was ordained, and in the fall of 1997, Danny Croce returned to prison, the very same prison, in fact, in which he had been incarcerated.

But this time he returned to be the prison chaplain.

At the same Network for Life meeting, there was Don, who had once been the most feared inmate in the California prison system. I met Don in prison; as it turned out, he was one of the plotters of a prison riot. Their aim was to take me hostage. Instead, he listened to me preach the gospel that day and gave his life to Christ. Don, after his release from prison, spent fifteen years working with disadvantaged children in the Dallas, Texas, area. Eighteen months ago, he went home to be with the Lord and to receive his crown.

And there was Mary Kay, who had been a bank robber. But after she was released from prison, she began to work to bring Christmas gifts to the children of inmates. Mary Kay was the person who began our Angel Tree program, which has now spread around the world.

And so it went around the room, case after case of men and women whom society would have written off as hopeless but who instead had been transformed by the power of the gospel. I hope it does not sound triumphalistic, but I know of no philosophy, no therapy, no psychology, no religion apart from Christianity that can provide for the transformation of the human will. What was bent toward sin by the Fall is now bent toward God.

CULTURAL TRANSFORMATION

But if we are to deal with the root causes of crime and are to promote a just society, we need to get to the causes of cultural collapse and discover ways to answer Novak's question of how we can encourage virtue. This means transforming cultures, and the place to begin is at the beginning, the family. To address this aspect adequately, I want briefly to explore the social role of the family.

In 1960, 9 percent of American children lived in single-parent homes; today that number is 36 percent, a fourfold increase.[4] This collapse of the family is at the heart of the cultural collapse and is one of the great curses of modern times. Study after study points to it as the chief contributing cause not only to crime but to many other pathologies. According to Kevin and Karen Wright of the State University of New York, research linking single-parent homes with delinquency and poverty began back in the early nineteenth century, and the link still holds in research today.[5]

Consider these statistics: Children in single-parent families are six times more likely to be poor, and half of the single mothers in the United States live below the poverty line. Children of divorce suffer intense grief, which often lasts for many years. Even as young adults, they are nearly twice as likely to require psychological help. Children from broken homes have more academic and behavioral problems at school and are nearly twice as likely to drop out of high school.[6] Girls in single-parent homes are at much greater risk for promiscuous sexuality and are three times more likely to have a child out of wedlock.[7]

Crime and substance abuse are strongly linked to fatherless households. Studies show that 60 percent of rapists grew up in fatherless homes, as did 72 percent of adolescent murderers and 70 percent of all long-term prison inmates. In a fourteen-year study (1979 to 1993) of 60,000 males, ages fourteen to twenty-two, Drs. Cynthia Harper and Sara McLanahan found that boys who grew up in fatherless homes are twice as likely to be incarcerated. The boys who grew up with a stepfather are three times more likely to be incarcerated.[8]

Rebuilding the family is a formidable task because the traditional family is under assault. It is threatened with an overthrow packaged as a mere "revision of definitions." Human beings will always pair off in unorthodox ways, but society as a whole must never normalize any form of "family" other than the traditional one of one man and one woman, united with intention of permanency, prepared for childbearing and childrearing. Sometimes defending the family will require us to risk being seen as negative or as "anti" something, but it can also take very positive forms. In this regard, I salute the Fatherhood Initiative, a publicity campaign by several American profamily organizations to promote respect for fatherhood and for the father's role in the family and in society. Promise Keepers—a nationwide movement of Christian men who publicly confess their failures to live up to their ideals and commit themselves to doing better—is another sign of positive activism. Promise Keepers events are often picketed by people who think the traditional family is oppressive—a sure sign that this movement has hit a nerve.

Then there was former Vice President Dan Quayle. Back when he was still vice president, he put his public career on the line with a strong speech about the decline of family values. At first he was mocked and scorned, and some even blamed him for George Bush's re-election loss in 1992. But a few months later *Atlantic Monthly*, one of the arbiters of upper-class intellectual respectability, ran a cover proclaiming in huge letters "Dan Quayle Was Right." The article behind the headline gave details on the weakening of the American family and the social disasters—including increases in crime—that this has brought about.[9] Now the arguments advanced in the Quayle speech are generally accepted as legitimate and sensible.

But it's one thing to acknowledge that a speech was right; it's another to bring about the necessary cultural changes. Our young people are still immersed in a culture of parental absence or neglect. They listen to music that glorifies violence, and they watch movies and play video games that chip away at the natural human instinct against killing other human beings.

A hundred years ago, even fifty years ago, if a child's family failed to discharge its responsibilities of moral training, other institutions could act as fail-safe substitutes. The free common schools may not have been perfect, but they taught the basics, including good citizenship. Then there were institutions such as the Boy Scouts. Today our educational establishment has become riddled with the relativism that I described earlier. And this, I must add, applies to the *good* schools; the rest define success as a full day without any shootings. As for the Boy Scouts, they are fighting for their survival in the wake of a recent New Jersey Supreme Court ruling that ordered the Scouts not to exclude homosexuals from serving as scoutmasters. The Supreme Court, in a 5-4 ruling, affirmed the right of the Boy Scouts not to allow homosexuals to serve as scoutmasters.[10]

We desperately need a renewal of these intermediate structures of society, what Edmund Burke called the "little platoons"—the neighborhood groups and clubs, the associations, and, of course, the church—to bolster the work of families in the transformation of our communities.

Then there is popular culture. A couple of generations ago, our culture may not have been strictly wholesome, but at least it did not exalt gangster life and brutalization of women. Movies may have pushed the envelope in some respects back in the 1950s, but they didn't show barnyard sex or severed body parts, as many of them routinely do today.

This litany of ills—so often articulated by William Bennett, Robert Bork, and other conservative thinkers—may sound like a simplistic conservative call for a return to the "good old days." To me, it points to something much more radical. We don't need restoration as much as we need transformation in our communities and our institutions, which shape popular cultural values.

It is vitally important that we transform neighborhoods so that people feel it's worth their while to care about their communities as well as about themselves, where people don't feel they have to huddle behind their walls to keep away from the bullets. For the dominant values of a neighborhood shape its behavior. Independent studies have shown that crime is lowest in areas that have the most churches, and highest in areas that have the most bars and liquor stores.[11]

And as we will see clearly in part 4, external order is a powerful symbol of legal and moral order. This was proved by an extensive study of crime and juvenile delinquency. Conducted jointly by Harvard University, the University of Chicago, and the Kaiser Institute, this survey studied 382 neighborhoods in Chicago, across a range of ethnic and economic characteristics. Conventional demographics turned out to explain nothing: Some neighborhoods with high minority populations had high crime rates; others had low ones. Some poor neighborhoods had high crime rates; others did not. There was only one reliable predictor of whether a community would be low-crime or high-crime: Whether it had, or lacked, a strong sense of community values and a willingness to impose those values on public space— what researchers called "community cohesion."

The study showed that crime was low in neighborhoods where neighbors felt free to discipline other people's children if those children skipped school or wrote on walls or wasted time on street corners. This may not be good news to those who place the "right to be left alone" above all other rights and to those who think children should have full adult rights in all matters. A reporter for the *Boston Globe*, a very liberal newspaper, put it somewhat ruefully in comments on the Chicago study: Safe neighborhoods, it seems, depend on "such things as being willing to look after other people's children and mind others' business."[12]

CHRISTIANITY'S ROLE
IN TRANSFORMATION

WE HAVE AN urgent task to restore the sense of community
cohesion and build a virtuous character into our common life.
Without individual virtue, we cannot achieve a virtuous culture.
As Michael Novak has trenchantly observed, "This country ought
to have, when it is healthy and when it is working as it is intended
to work, 250 million policemen—called *conscience.*" He continues,
"When there are 250 million consciences on guard, it is surprising
how few police are needed on the streets."[1] Without a virtuous
culture, we cannot hire enough police to keep order.

It may be asked why secular societies cannot—or do not—undertake on purely secular grounds reforms such as I have suggested. Sometimes they do. But I don't think a secular worldview will ever sustain a widespread, ongoing experiment in the restoration of a truly peaceful community, what the Old Testament would call *shalom*. If we were to see such an attempt on a secular basis, it would swiftly turn into statism—an imposition of authority by an all-powerful government. This is what is happening with the communitarian movement, which tries to create a sense of community, but it does so without any understanding of God's role in the true community. As a result, the movement's efforts often turn out to be just the old welfare-state liberalism under a patina of communitarian oratory. After all, the American left learned long ago in the 1930s to use the rhetoric of family, community, and justice to sponsor the emergence of a bureaucratic megastate that saps authentic community spirit and interferes with legitimate civil liberties more often than does the occasional rogue police officer. The communitarians are trying to do a Christian thing in a non-Christian way. It won't work that way because it doesn't get to the heart of the matter—transformation.

This is why it is so vitally important that the church, that is, Christian people, take the lead not only in presenting the gospel and therefore producing individual transformation, but also in reanimating the culture, bringing Christian truth to bear in all aspects of our common lives together. Historically this has been the role of the Christian church; this is why the great historian Christopher Dawson called the church the "soul" of Western civilization. All the more in today's relativistic culture must the church assert its role if virtue is to be exalted and encouraged.

During a visit to the Brazilian Humaita prison, the first prison run as a Christian prison, I saw in a very graphic way the essence of what I've attempted to say here: The Christian understanding of life provides the one sure basis for the transformation of individuals and cultures. Only the gospel provides the real power to do this.

Humaita is a remarkable place, an old prison that had been closed by the authorities of the state of Sao Paulo twenty-five years ago and promptly reopened at the urging of two men who were active in the Cursillo movement, a Catholic evangelization program. One man was a lawyer, the other a judge. They promised the state that they would run the prison as a Christian institution, the state providing only the facility and food. For more than twenty-five years they did so (until the ancient structure was closed last year, its work now being replicated in other institutions).

Entering Humaita was an experience. Instead of seeing the usual gray, dingy walls, I was met by a clean, almost inviting atmosphere. The prison had a well-tended garden with signs prominent everywhere, most of them taken from the Psalms or Proverbs, some of them with superb admonitions about the love of God being the essence of true justice. I was met this day at the gate, as I have been at every visit since, by a guard who was actually an inmate. In this instance, the guard was a convicted murderer, swinging a huge chain of keys from his belt. When inmates arrived at Humaita, their chains were removed, and they were told that in this prison they are constrained not by steel but by the love of Christ.

Everywhere I walked through the prison, I saw men with smiles. The living areas were spotlessly clean, the beds well made. Again, huge posters hung over the work area. I remember one that read: "He who lives by killing time, dies with it." The men at work on their crafts or industrial projects seemed joyous, fulfilled. I was there at mealtime, and as the food was delivered, the men all stood and recited the Lord's Prayer before eating. The chapel services were filled to overflowing with singing, joyous worship, and moving testimonies.

The secret of the Humaita concept is not only that every prisoner is matched up with an outside volunteer who takes a personal interest in that individual, not only that the Bible is taught by ministers and priests night after night, not only that people work with joy, but it is in the *totality* of the experience that has been created at Humaita and at the other prisons like it. It is a Christian culture, and the prisoners are immersed in it. And what we have learned over all of these years is that when people live in a Christian culture—when the basic presuppositions about their life are Christian, when the teaching is Christian, when the values that are shared in common are Christian—people begin to behave "christianly" (Psalm 66:1-3). It is a wonderful metaphor for our culture at large. And, of course, none of it is imposed. All of the inmates as well as the workers volunteer to be in this program.

The essence of it was captured for me as I was getting ready to leave after my first visit a decade ago. One of the inmates asked if I would like to see the punishment cells, where people in this old prison had been kept as a form of torture. He told me that there was one inmate in one punishment cell.

I assured him I would like to do this. He paused and asked again if I was certain I was ready. I was a bit offended; hadn't I been in solitary confinement and segregation cells in Perm Camp 35 in Russia and some of the worst holes in the world? "Of course," I said impatiently, "let's go."

The inmate led me down a long corridor with both solid steel and barred doors on either side until we came to the end where there was one locked solid steel door. The inmate slowly took out his keys and turned the lock. Then he opened the slot, looked inside, turned to me, and said, "Yes, he's in there. Are you sure you want to go in?"

By now I was thoroughly impatient. "Of course, open the door." As he swung open the door, I could see a table with a lamp on it and some books, and then as I turned and walked into the cell, I looked to the right, and there on the wall was a beautifully hand-carved crucifix, Christ hanging on the cross.

The inmate turned to me and said, "That's him, that's the inmate here in solitary. He's doing the time for us."

That reality, the reality of the gospel, is the *only* life-transforming, indeed culture-transforming power. In that is the answer not just to crime but also to life's greatest dilemma.

PART FOUR

JUSTICE THAT RESTORES

RESTORATIVE JUSTICE

WE REALIZE THAT crime and social pathologies will never be eliminated. But Christians believe that individuals and cultures can be redeemed, that individuals who break both the law and the community's peace can be restored. Which brings me to the subject at hand: justice that restores or, as many choose to call it, restorative justice.

The term *restorative justice* was probably first used by the American scholar Albert Eglash. In a 1977 article, he described three types of criminal justice: (1) retributive justice, which is based on punishment, (2) distributive justice, which is based on therapeutic treatment of offenders, and (3) restorative justice, which is based on restitution or to some extent making right the wrongs done.[1] My able associates

Daniel Van Ness and Karen Strong, who have pioneered concepts of restorative justice, define the third option this way: "Restorative justice focuses on repairing the harm caused by crime and reducing the likelihood of future harm."[2]

In Britain the term *relational justice* is often used to describe the kind of justice that restores. Through the superb work done by the Relationships Foundation and particularly Michael Schluter, Jonathan Burnside, and Nicola Baker, the Relational Justice Initiative has been established. In *Relational Justice* Jonathan Burnside offers three views somewhat parallel to those described by Eglash. He contrasts the "antiseptic" view of justice, that is, the cold application of law, with a "passionate" understanding of justice, which emphasizes compassion and protection of the weak.[3] But a full view of justice, Burnside contends, "is about more than [either] due process" or "compassion"; he writes, "Above all it reflects our desire to live in right relationship."[4] Burnside and his colleagues argue very convincingly that true justice involves an ongoing dialectic between the antiseptic and compassionate views, aiming higher to achieve the goal of right relationships. But this dialectic can take place only within the context of what moral philosopher Alasdair MacIntyre calls a "tradition of enquiry." That tradition, in Burnside's view and mine, is Christianity, which introduced to Western thought the idea of seeing humanity in relational terms—in relationships between God and humans and in relationships among humans.

Relational justice as we articulate it—not all views of restorative justice are rooted in a Christian worldview—grounds justice ultimately in the relationships flowing from God to humans. Restorative justice grounds justice in the peace of God's created order. Both relational and restorative justice, therefore, offer aspects of the biblical view of *shalom*, a peace that is intrinsically relational and righteous.

Understanding the concept of *shalom* is most helpful in understanding restorative justice. Modern Israelis may often use the word glibly as a greeting, but to the biblical Hebrews it meant something much more profound. It meant peace, but not simply the absence of hostilities; it meant true harmony and concord, people living together in the right order that God intended. *Shalom* is a state in which everything is well, complete, and present.

We see in the biblical perspective that *shalom* is a reflection of God's very character, of his righteousness. This theme is threaded through Scripture. The Hebrew term for *righteousness* is *tsedeq,* which means conformity to a standard. Psalm 23 tells us that the Lord leads his sheep along *tsedeq* paths—paths that are safe and walkable, paths of righteousness that lead to green pastures. In the context of law, *tsedeq* came to stand for the abstract behavioral standard that we are to observe before God and with each other.[5] But Scripture usually links *tsedeq* with other words related to justice and peace. Take Psalm 85:10: "Steadfast love and faithfulness will meet; righteousness *[tsedeq]* and peace *[shalom]* will kiss each other" (RSV). The relational aspects of *tsedeq* can be clearly seen in this psalm.

I contend that a biblical worldview is the only one that can produce a system of true justice, one that holds *individuals responsible* for their actions (that is, fallen individuals have a moral duty) under an objective *rule of law* (which we believe is rooted in revelation) but always in the *context of community* and always with the *chance of transformation of the individual* and *the healing of fractured relationships and of the moral order.*

As previously noted, when justice is not realized, when the system fails to achieve its promised results, it is because one of these elements—individual responsibility under law but in the context of community, individual transformation, and healing of relationships— is neglected or thrown out of balance. The Pharisees, for example, had a high view of the law but no tolerance for the kind of grace and transformation that Jesus offered to wayward individuals; modern liberals, on the other hand, have extolled the importance of community all too well but often at the expense of individual responsibility.

CRIME IS THE COMMUNITY'S BUSINESS

The term *restorative justice* and these concepts may seem novel and original only because we have lived the past fifty years under either the retributive (punishment) or distributive (therapeutic) models, both of which in many respects removed criminal justice from the concern of the community. Justice has become clinical and detached, solely the function of the institutions. But it wasn't always this way. Historically it was understood that achieving justice involved more than police and prosecutors reacting to major transgressions.

William Wilberforce, for example, the great evangelical British statesman and personal model for my life, once wrote that "the most effectual way to prevent the greater crimes is by punishing the smaller, and by endeavoring to repress the general spirit of licentiousness, which is the parent of every kind of vice."[6] This was a philosophy derived from the biblical view of communal order, and it was the same philosophy that influenced the original principles of policing laid out by Wilberforce's contemporary Sir Robert Peel, who served as home secretary when the Metropolitan Police of London was established in 1829. The first job of the police, Peel argued, was not fighting crime but keeping peace, and he established high standards of professionalism as the police worked to prevent crime. (Indicative of his influence is the fact that the term *bobby,* used for police, came from Peel's Christian name.)

Seventy years later in the New York City Charter, the same principles were repeated: "It is hereby made the duty of the police department to especially preserve the public peace, . . . remove all nuisances in the public streets, . . . restrain all unlawful and disorderly conduct."[7]

Not surprisingly then, in the United States at the turn of the last century it was the police who developed food and soup lines, built police stations with space where migrants could stay, referred beggars to charitable agencies, returned lost children to their homes, and patrolled the streets, preserving the good order of the community.

This view of policing and criminal justice began to unravel in the 1960s. This was due in part to the emergence of the drug culture and the rapid urbanization of modern societies. But it was due as well to a distinct change in our view of police responsibilities. In the 1970s and 1980s, court decisions repeatedly struck down statutes against vagrancy and loitering, statutes that had been passed to uphold public order. Before long, streets, parks, and subways in major urban areas were filled with beggars, prostitutes, drunks, and homeless people. Compounding the problem, there was at the very same time a massive movement to deinstitutionalize the mentally ill and a rise in drug-related crimes. Cities became like combat zones.

In 1982 social scientists James Q. Wilson and George L. Kelling wrote a landmark article describing what they called the broken-window theory.[8] They argued that if a building is left in disrepair with a window broken, for example, soon all the windows are knocked out. Or if a car is sitting on the street badly dented or with broken windows, in a matter of hours the car is destroyed by vandals. Graffiti and litter similarly send a message that authorities are unwilling or are unable to enforce standards of decent behavior. Kelling and Wilson argued that reversing that process would create an attitude of public order, an attitude that would discourage crimes.

In the early 1990s the New York police chief took the broken-window theory to heart and persuaded New York's newly elected mayor and tough ex-prosecutor, Rudolph Giuliani, to give the theory a try. Orders went out to Precincts 69 and 75 and to Brooklyn to "fix broken windows," arrest petty offenders, and clean up neighborhoods. The police were to adopt zero tolerance for any violation of public order. Whereas before they had ignored turnstile jumping at subways, officers now nabbed the offenders who often as not turned out to be muggers. Whereas before they had turned a blind eye to minor traffic violations, officers now stopped all violators, which often led to the discovery of drugs and guns in the cars. In Precinct 75, for example, which once had been one of the most dangerous places in America, homicides dropped from 129 to 47 over a three-year period.[9]

Civil libertarians attacked these crime-prevention programs, relying on the very same Supreme Court decisions that had hamstrung the police in going after vagrants and vagabonds. But this time the police drafted their statutes carefully to penalize behavior, not status, and the courts began backing the police.

Cities around the country imitated New York, with dramatic results. Following Commissioner Bratton's work in New York, Philadelphia Police Commissioner John Timoney applied the broken-window theory; for him it was a life-changing discovery. He later said, "I spent 29 years in the New York City police department, and I spent the first 25 years doing everything wrong."[10]

Politicians were quick to trumpet their successes anywhere they could find a microphone, as if they had discovered the Holy Grail, the long-sought answer to crime. Yet all they had discovered was the well-established fundamental, biblical truth of *shalom*, which has informed church thought through the centuries. It was most powerfully articulated in the fourth century by Saint Augustine in his classic *City of God*. Augustine taught that peace is the "tranquillity produced by order" *(tranquillitas ordinis)*. A community, Augustine argued, enjoys peace and harmony only when it follows the created moral order; only an ordered civil life allows fallen human beings to live and work together.[11]

We find ourselves back to that stubborn truth that just will not go away: When we order our lives according to God's created physical and moral order, we can live peacefully and rationally. When we deny that created moral order, we live in chaos. The biblical worldview provides a basis for true justice. It provides a basis for restoring to order the disorder that crime and other social pathologies create.

ELEMENTS OF
RESTORATIVE JUSTICE

WHAT DOES RESTORATIVE justice look like in practice? Let's see how it fleshes itself out in prevention programs, sentencing options, reintegration of the offenders into the community, and the treatment of the crime victims.

PREVENTION PROGRAMS

First, it seems self-evident that any enlightened policy would work to keep the *shalom* from being broken in the first place. So policy makers and communities should look for ways to prevent the crimes that

break the *shalom* or destroy the tranquil order. This involves the restoration of a moral climate that encourages virtue.

It further calls for the philosophy first articulated by Sir Robert
Peel, who understood the need to preserve order at all levels. This is,
of course, what Commissioner Bratton discovered in New York by
arresting minor offenders, cleaning up the streets, and creating an
environment that discouraged more serious crimes. Fixing "broken
windows" sends the right message.

Even modest proactive police work can achieve great success.
In Charleston, South Carolina, a police chief took an innovative
approach to drug dealers. Police watched people on the street
corners and noted teenagers who stopped whatever they were doing
and appeared to be talking harmlessly when the police drove by.
The police *knew* they were dealers who would resume their dealing
as soon as they drove away. So the chief ordered the police to get
out of their cars, approach the kids, and take their pictures with
cameras. That's all they did, but soon the dealers would move to
another area, and the camera-toting cops followed them. In time,
many of the dealers were shut down.[1]

And it is not just policing that needs to change. Prosecution and
courts should also become increasingly localized so that they are ready
and able to address local situations. Judge Christopher Compston, a
British circuit judge who is active in Prison Fellowship, has proposed
what he calls local courts, local judges, and local sentencing. He
argues that these courts should convene local committees to meet to
discuss matters of community concern. Such committees could not
only help the judges understand local concerns but also begin to
address those matters.[2]

In America we have twelve community courts already in operation,
and thirteen more will be added. The newest community court,
Red Hook Community Justice Center, opened in the heart of a low-

income neighborhood in Brooklyn, New York. Instead of waiting for crimes to occur, the community court supports local residents not only in "doing justice" with a variety of innovative programs in crime prevention but also in resolving problems *before* the offenders go to court. The court is set up to hear low-level criminal, family, and civil cases. The community court offers job training, runs a restitution program, provides drug treatment, and gives mental health counseling. These initiatives help reinforce the notion of individual responsibility.[3]

Police can also work with community groups, those intermediate structures so important to the peace of the community and a key to preventing crime. Police in Dallas, Texas, for example, achieved a 26 percent drop in juvenile crime through a gang-intervention program sponsored by seventeen civic groups. Workers reached 3,000 young people in one year with education, recreation, and job-training programs.[4] The Dallas police chief acknowledged that at one time he believed police alone could handle crime, but he now realizes that he needs to work with the community.

The community needs to get involved early in the lives of young people. These kinds of efforts pay off. The National Ten-Point Leadership Foundation, led by the Reverend Eugene F. Rivers III of Boston, a former Philadelphia gang member, has matched responsible adults with thousands of at-risk youths and helped to spark ecumenical, interfaith, and public-private partnerships dedicated to reducing violence in cities all across the country.[5]

In efforts at prevention, intervention programs that divert young offenders from prison are another valuable resource, particularly sparing kids from beginning the vicious cycle of prison, release, rearrest, prison, and on and on. And these interventions work.

Take the case of Tony, who had a reputation as a troublemaker in a neighborhood infested by drug dealers. Tony was on probation for car theft.

But Tony got a break through a program called Choice, which takes an unconventional approach. It's part of an intensive, supervised probation in which a caseworker checks on Tony several times a day. Tony's caseworker, a young college graduate, knocks on Tony's door every morning and makes sure he gets off to school. He tutors Tony after school, takes him to doctors' appointments, and arranges basketball games with other kids.[6]

In the Choice program, every teen has to sign a contract agreeing to specific behavioral goals such as going to school, keeping a curfew, cooperating with parents. And caseworkers are there to hold the kids to their contracts. If the teens don't keep their curfew, their caseworker goes out looking for them.

The Choice program is committed to helping troubled kids stay with their families and stay *out* of institutions. And it has a great record: Since it began in 1989, more than 80 percent of its teens have remained free of arrest. And those rearrested have been charged with less serious offenses. The Choice program is cost effective: In the juvenile system, costs range from $40,000 to $60,000 a year per person, but the average cost in the Choice program is $6,000 a year. The program has already been replicated in San Diego, California, as well as Hartford, Connecticut.

Prison Fellowship in the United States, Great Britain, and around the world has discovered just how important it is to work with kids *before* they become offenders. We are involved in two volunteer programs that are proving to be very effective.

The first is Angel Tree. Each year, Prison Fellowship volunteers and staff go through the prisons asking inmates if they would like someone to deliver a gift to their children in their name at Christmastime. The response from the inmates is overwhelming. Last year in the United States, we reached 500,000 kids with more than 100,000 volunteers purchasing and wrapping gifts, locating the caregivers, and then actually making the deliveries.

But Angel Tree isn't simply bringing gifts to kids. The volunteers often share the message of redemption with the families and bring other tangible help. And as the program matures, more and more volunteers are going back, taking an ongoing interest in the kids all year round. This past summer, churches sent nearly 8,000 Angel Tree kids to Christian camps. Nothing warms my heart more than the stories we've heard of young kids giving their lives to Christ, some even leading their incarcerated parents to the Lord. Thousands of kids are being delivered from the vicious cycle of crime and prison.

This is truly a remarkable opportunity for the church to do something major to prevent crime. James Q. Wilson, America's leading criminologist, says that a leading predictor of future criminal behavior is to have a mother or father in prison.[7] Experts project that children with parents in prison are six times more likely than other kids to commit a crime.[8]

The second program, which is expanding in America, is called MatchPoint, which matches trained Christian adults with kids who are at high risk. The program helps keep the mentoring relationships on course through the inevitable ups and downs that come because of the tough defenses of the kids and the issues they face at school, in court, and in their families. Mentors are mature Christian adults who commit themselves to a long-term relationship that demonstrates the unconditional love of Jesus Christ. As kids bond with their mentors, their worldview begins to open up to include new values and choices learned through respect and love—replacing the anger and alienation that is so typical of troubled kids.

We know that mentoring programs work. A recent Big Brothers/ Big Sisters study found that "youngsters matched with mentors are

46 percent less likely to use drugs, 27 percent less likely to begin drinking, one-third less likely to commit assault, and half as likely to skip school."[9]

Efforts like these are urgently needed. Juvenile offenses have been soaring since the mid-1980s. Although crime rates among young people have seen some recent declines—due, I believe, to changes in policing and demographics as well as a multitude of community efforts targeting at-risk kids—violent crime remains stubbornly high. In 1998 it was still three and a half times higher than it was in 1961.[10]

But if we are alarmed by gang violence and juvenile crime today, the demographic projections should really sober us: The number of fourteen- to seventeen-year-olds will be 20 percent greater in 2005 than it was in 1996; by 2006, America will have 30 million teenagers. By the year 2010, the number of juveniles is projected to increase by 31 percent. And we know from experience that this is the group that is producing the most savage and dangerous crimes.[11]

When we find ways to turn this tide, we will not only improve lives and enhance public security but also save huge investments of public funds. A study in Minnesota found that preventing just five people from committing violent crimes saves the state $4 million in prison and corrections costs. Just think how many people could be reached with that same money spent on preventative programs.[12]

Clearly there is a great opportunity here for intermediate structures such as churches and community groups to perform a great service and to provide a wonderful witness in the process. This is by far the most effective role we can play. As two well-regarded social scientists wrote, "The best defense against crime is not a thin blue line but a community of individuals respectful of others."[13] And revitalizing these "little platoons" is crucial for reasons beyond simply their impact on criminal justice. They are one of the greatest resources for promoting a healthy social order, which both prevents crime in the first instance and helps heal its effect when it occurs.

These intermediate structures, it is important to remember, provide the great leavening and humanizing influence in any culture. The grave danger of the modern technocratic society is that these structures have been weakened as an all-powerful, therapeutic nanny state has taken over all aspects of welfare and policy responses to human needs. This is the very danger Hannah Arendt, the political philosopher who fled from Nazi Germany, so eloquently warned against as a precursor to tyranny. Revitalizing these structures is therefore a high-priority task for communities, and the church should be in the vanguard. We, of all people, understand how essential this is to the right ordering of society, that is, to *shalom*.

SENTENCING: PRISONS AND ALTERNATIVES

A second principle of restorative justice is its wise sentencing practices. Of practical concern to any sound—and I would add biblical—justice system is making judicious use of prisons. We have not done this in our country.

The Magnitude of the Problem

As previously noted, today there are 2 million people in prison or jail in the United States, the second highest rate of incarceration per capita in the world. And consider these chilling statistics: One out of twenty Americans born in 1999 will serve time in prison, according to a U.S. Department of Justice study. For blacks, the projection is one out of four. By 1996, 8.3 percent of all black men aged twenty-five to twenty-nine were in prison.[14]

Why is this so? What has been the cause of this incredible explosion in prison population? The excessive use of prison is the result of the flawed view of human nature and mistaken notions about the causes of crime, as discussed in part 2. We have crammed hundreds of thousands of offenders into prisons in the mistaken idea that prison will deter crime or rehabilitate the offender. (Yes, there is, I acknowledge, a deterrent effect in some cases, and yes, some people are rehabilitated in prison, although it is not *because* of prison.)

The truth is that prisons are primarily good for incapacitating dangerous offenders, those convicted of violent or dangerous crimes. It is rather like a hospital quarantine ward, where people with communicable diseases are kept apart to protect others.

The problem is that prisons are filled with many people who are not dangerous to society and do not need to be quarantined; in fact, offenders often become hardened in their criminal disposition because of the experience.

We must revamp our current policies and find noncustodial alternatives. This can safely be done for large numbers of offenders who are not dangerous. In 1995, 71 percent of those sentenced to state prisons were convicted of nonviolent offenses.[15]

Drug-related convictions have literally flooded our prisons with mostly nondangerous offenders. To illustrate the dreadful human cost as well as the financial burdens we have created, consider the case of Gloria Van Winkle, who is currently in the seventh year of a life sentence for possessing forty dollars' worth of cocaine. Sentenced under a statute mandating a life sentence for a third offense, Mrs. Van Winkle passes her days just waiting for visits from her children, ages seven and eleven. "I can't laugh anymore. I can't cry," she says. "It's just a low rage that makes me numb." (Three-fourths of the 54,000 women jailed for drug offenses have children.)[16]

The *New York Times*, in a shocking exposé early in 1999, discovered hundreds of prisoners like Mrs. Van Winkle. One woman, for example, with no criminal record was serving ten years for mailing a package for a friend, who paid her forty-four dollars; the package just happened to contain drugs. Another first offender, a fifty-five-year-old father of nine children, a man with no prior convictions, is serving a mandatory five-year sentence for growing 141 marijuana plants.[17] Draconian sentencing practices—particularly mandatory minimum sentences or so-called "three-time loser" statutes—have contributed to the exploding prison population.

When I was a prisoner, I saw how these policies devastate human lives. I ran the washing machine in the prison laundry. The man who ran the dryer was the former chairman of the board of the American Medical Association. Under prison regulations, I was not allowed to practice law, and he was not allowed to practice medicine. This man was being eaten away with bitterness and anger. I stayed in touch with him after his release from prison, and he never fully recovered from the experience. Similarly a young drug offender who was converted in prison and with whom I stayed in close touch found the incarceration experience so devastating that he was unable to sustain stable personal relationships later. A former banker incarcerated with me for $3,000 of tax evasion spent the rest of his life trying to recover his lost reputation.

Some of those who were involved in Watergate with me—I think of John Ehrlichman and John Mitchell in particular—were to their last days bitter, angry, broken men. Prison, no matter how modern the institution or how many amenities are available, is the harshest of punishments. There is nothing quite like watching the hands of the clock not move. I can remember some days in prison looking at the clock, seeing that it was nine in the morning. I read, studied, worked at my laundry job, and several hours later, or so I thought, I looked at the clock again to discover that it was nine-thirty. Time stands still in prison.

In my dormitory were a handful of serious criminals, most of them doing the tail end of long sentences. They were the best behaved and

actually the best adjusted. They had spent years in solitary confinement or in cold, forbidding cellblocks. They were men who had
committed violent crimes, and they knew their prison term was justified. But most of the others were there for minor offenses: writing
bad checks, making illegal alcohol, minor drug dealing and using,
petty embezzling. At a staggering cost in public funds and human
degradation, we incarcerate thousands upon thousands of people
like this.

We need to target those who are dangerous. Criminologist James
Q. Wilson has reached a remarkable conclusion based on studies
worldwide: 50 percent of serious crimes are committed by 6 percent
of the offenders. And this 6 percent figure remained constant over
the years of his studies. So 6 percent of the boys of a given age group
commit more than half of the crimes committed in that age group;
and this is true, Wilson has concluded, whether we are talking about
Philadelphia, London, Copenhagen, or Orange County, California.[18]
It is self-evident that better police work and more selective prosecution aimed at the small percentage of busy young criminals could
greatly reduce the numbers of people filling our prisons with little
negative impact on crime rates or public safety.

Only nations that are both rich and foolish could possibly afford
to follow these policies. They do not work. Our recidivism rate is
approximately 75 percent in four years following release. (I suspect
in reality it might be higher. Whenever I'm in prison, I ask people
how many have been there before, and the vast majority of hands are
raised.) The rate today is the same as it was when prisons were half
the size they are today, which, if we follow the logic, leads inevitably
to the law of unintended consequences: the more people we put in
prison, the more crime we will have.

And indeed we are spending huge amounts of tax money on prisons, $30 billion in 1997.[19]

Many people are beginning to wake up to the mistakes we have made in filling prisons beyond their capacity. John DiIulio, formerly of Princeton University and now at the University of Pennsylvania, is one of the most respected young social scientists in America, best known of late for his studies on faith-based solutions to public-policy problems. DiIulio, who just a few years ago coined the phrase "super-predator" to describe the coming juvenile crime crisis, zealously advocated more prisons and harsher sentences. But, objective scholar that he is, he has now reversed his position entirely, arguing against mandatory minimum sentences and against further prison construction.[20]

Prisons That Work

Sadly, even under the best of conditions, there will always be a need for prisons for those who pose a danger to society. But even in those instances, we should work to make the prison experience as redemptive as possible. One way is to provide meaningful work. Idleness is one of the most debilitating aspects of prison life, as I so well remember from my own experience. People drift across the prison compound, stare vacantly at the walls of their cells, or watch TV incessantly. They become empty shells with nowhere to go, no work to perform. For days on end they feel they have no purpose.

Christians believe, and we intuitively understand, that humans are created in the image of God and that God created us for a purpose. This is part of the *imago Dei* or image of God within us. We are restless until we find and fulfill our purpose. When circumstances make it impossible for us to be productive, humans can go mad—quite literally. This was a point made by Fyodor Dostoyevsky in *The House of the Dead,* where he argued that if one wanted to crush a person utterly, one should simply give him work of a completely senseless, irrational nature. "If he had to move a heap of earth from one place to another

and back again—I believe the convict would hang himself . . . preferring rather to die than endure . . . such humiliation, shame and
torture."[21]

The commandant of the Nazi concentration camp in Hungary
during World War II obviously agreed with Dostoyevsky. He
instructed the guards to have prisoners shovel debris into carts and
drag it from one end of the factory compound to the other. Then
when the piles accumulated at the far end, the prisoners were ordered
to move them back. Day after day the prisoners shoved the same
mountain of rubble back and forth from one end of the camp to the
other. Earlier they had been working diligently to produce fuel that
was used by their hated captors against the Allies. Even though they
had been doing something to help the despised Nazis, they could
maintain some sanity and dignity. But deprived of work and purpose,
many attempted escape, running into the electrified fence only to
be electrocuted or shot by the guards. The commandant who had
ordered the experiment, after seeing the results, smugly remarked
that at this rate there would soon be "no more need to use the
crematorium."[22]

So real work programs—not make-work as I experienced, raking
leaves or starting machines of laundry in the morning and then sitting
eight hours and watching them—are vital, lest prison be a totally
destructive experience.

In the Chang Hi Prison in Singapore, for example, most of the
10,000 inmates are gainfully employed. Private industries come into
the prisons and bid to run electronics plants, manufacturing facilities,
bakeries, and the like. The inmates are employed at two-thirds the
going wage on the outside, and from their earnings they pay for their
room and board at the prison, make restitution, and contribute to the
support of their families on the outside. The overall industrial plan is
managed by a quasi-governmental agency known as SCORE, which

actually makes a profit for the prison system. I found the morale in that prison to be as good as I have found in any of the six hundred prisons I've visited around the world.

A British inspector of prisons reports the results of a review of British prisons with the recommendations that the concepts of a healthy prison be adopted. A healthy prison, according to the report, is one in which

- the weakest prisoners feel safe.
- all prisoners are treated with respect and as individuals.
- all prisoners are busily occupied, are expected to improve themselves, and are given the opportunity to do so.
- all prisoners can strengthen links with their family and prepare for release.[23]

This is a very commendable statement, a noble goal indeed, and one that should be honored in practice.

Community-Based Programs

But better than sentencing offenders to prison, even socially redemptive prisons, is sentencing them to community-based alternative programs. And the good news is that several programs like this do exist. In addition to diversion programs intended mostly for juveniles, there are a whole host of socially redemptive, lower cost alternative sanctions available.

Over the past several years, many states have passed community corrections statutes. In 1983, for example, Florida created a statewide program of community service, restitution, and other sanctions enforced by what became the nation's largest and most encompassing house-arrest and community-supervision program.

Offenders were sentenced, but they served their time at home, often wearing monitoring equipment such as electronic bracelets. The state imposed mandatory strict surveillance so that community-control officers had caseloads of no more than twenty offenders.

A study conducted in the first few years of the program revealed that between 50 and 65 percent of those in the program would otherwise have been sent to prisons, so the pressure on new prison construction was substantially alleviated, saving the state the equivalent of 7.5 prisons. The recidivism rate in the community program was only 27 percent, less than half the rate for prisons; and only one-third of the people who were sent back to prison were sent for new crimes. The program continues to be successful. Between 1993 and now, only 16 percent of those on electronic monitoring and house arrest in Florida had their probation revoked for new crimes committed within a two-year follow-up period.[24]

One of the most obvious prison alternatives, which comes under the general restorative-justice principle of reparation, is restitution. Most restitution programs require inmates to work at regular jobs so that they can pay back their victims or put money into a victim fund. In case after case we have heard how restitution profoundly affects the offender. Offenders repeatedly tell me that they had no appreciation of the damage they had done until they had to work to pay back the person wronged.

Let me give you one example of how restitution can work in practice. Joseph, a young teenager, stole $1,500 from his employer, who planned to prosecute. Joseph would have been convicted and sentenced to three years at a cost of $18,000 per year. Instead, Joseph's pastor sent a group of church elders to the judge, and they pleaded with him to let Joseph be assigned to a restitution program at the church. Several elders would see that he worked and that his wages were withheld. The judge agreed. The church elders gave Joseph a job, withheld money from his wages to pay back the person from whom he had stolen, and mentored Joseph through the process.

Not only did Joseph learn the true cost of what he had done, but he also experienced Christ's love in a transforming way. He is now coach of the church baseball team, a serious disciple who is now working to minister to others.

The judge was so impressed with the results that he asked the church to take responsibility for twenty more offenders.[25]

We know that programs such as these not only work to help repay victims but also to discourage crime. By taking responsibility for repaying their victims, offenders learn their lesson by a direct connection between the harm they caused and the punishment they received. Consider the alternative: going to prison to nurse their own sense of being victims. It makes sense that a study in South Carolina showed that counties with the best restitution-collection rates have the lowest crime rates.[26]

I'm always amused when I address political bodies—state legislatures, committees of the Congress, or parliamentary bodies around the world—recommending that offenders work to pay back their victims rather than occupying an expensive prison cell. Invariably politicians will tell me afterward that restitution sounds like a wonderful idea. When they ask where it came from, I have a standard reply. I ask them if they have a Bible, which most acknowledge they do. I then suggest that they read Exodus 21 and 22; I also suggest the story of Zacchaeus in Luke 19. Restitution is precisely the biblical answer to crime, and it works because it makes offenders responsible to make some kind of direct amends to those they have wronged.

There are countless other alternative programs such as supervised probation and work-release programs. Not all of these will be suitable for all cases, but programs like these are going to be increasingly necessary if we are to avoid the high cost of incarceration and find community-based punishments that are tailored to the offense.

REINTEGRATION

In addition to creating prevention programs and providing effective sentencing options, restorative justice must provide a third foundation: opportunity for the offender to be reintegrated into society when he or she comes out of prison. The place to begin the reintegration process is in prison, where inmates can be prepared for their eventual return to society.

One of the programs of Prison Fellowship U.S.A. is called Life Plan Seminars. Near the end of the prisoners' time in prison, they are invited to attend a long weekend seminar in which they go over all the basics they'll need to plan for life on the outside. We forget that someone who has been incarcerated for a long time may not even know how to balance a checkbook or attend to what we consider the most basic tasks of life. We have been told prisoners have found these seminars to be enormously helpful. In addition, in the InnerChange Freedom Initiative, a prison unit run by Prison Fellowship in the states of Texas and Iowa, inmates are required to attend extensive courses on transition into civilian life. During these courses, they are matched with mature Christian people who agree to mentor them when they are released.

Communities must work with offenders to help them overcome the obstacles they face as they make the transition from prison to the community. The key to reintegration, one of the most critical elements of restorative justice, is the ability of the church to marshal volunteer resources to mentor and encourage inmates when they return to the community.

Mentoring, we have discovered, is critical to reducing recidivism. I was taken to visit a bus stop in south central Los Angeles, one of the areas most severely affected by urban blight. Every Friday night buses would arrive from the various state penitentiaries and dump ex-offenders into the streets. Before most of the men and women could walk to their homes or families, they were approached by drug dealers and prostitutes. The recidivism process started when they were only steps away from the prison bus. These men and women should have been met at the bus stop by church volunteers, and that is now beginning to happen.

In a model Prison Fellowship aftercare program called Detroit TOP (an acronym standing for Transition of Prisoners), we accept inmates who are coming back to urban Detroit from Michigan state prisons. Every one of the inmates is mentored by a mature Christian and "adopted" by a participating church.

TOP admits only those who are at high risk of returning to prison; 98 percent of TOP participants have had serious drug- or alcohol-abuse problems, and most have been to prison several times. When participants enter TOP, the first step is a thirty-day mandatory orientation program. They are then assigned to mentors, provided by one of the thirty-two churches that actively support TOP. Each participant works with TOP staff to create a transition plan that includes ways to overcome the person's toughest obstacles to successful transition. In addition to the mentoring, participants attend weekly support and accountability meetings that are firmly rooted in Scripture.

In six years of operation, TOP has proven that it works. Less than one percent of TOP graduates have returned to prison for committing a new crime. That compares to national recidivism statistics of approximately 75 percent.

Admittedly, this is an intensive one-on-one effort that requires a great commitment. It is daunting to think that this might be replicated so that a mentor would be available for every inmate being released. But the real question is, Why not?

INVOLVING THE CRIME VICTIM

A fourth foundational element of restorative justice is the recognition that crime victims are an essential consideration in the response to crime. One way for victims to participate meaningfully in the criminal justice process is through what is known as "encounter programs." These are opportunities for victims (if they so choose) to interact with offenders in a carefully prepared setting for the purpose of addressing the harm caused by the crime. This provides a tremendous catharsis for victims—the ones who have been wronged.

Many victims feel a seething rage that they have been violated in their person or their property, and yet they're neglected, simply used as the tool of the prosecutors for the state. It's as if the victims haven't been offended against. An essential ingredient in justice is thus lost: the actual and real nature of the wrong and its consequences for people's lives.

From offenders' standpoint, the antiseptic and procedural emphasis on justice as a matter of legal maneuvering, detached from real people, can undermine offenders' sense of responsibility for their crimes. They come to believe they have committed a crime against the state, and the state will prosecute them. And they seldom give any thought at all to their victims.

I was moved by the description Peter Walker, Prison Fellowship's director for England and Wales, gives of the nineteen-year-old burglar who, when he went into a home, turned around the pictures of the people of the home so he didn't have to look at the faces of those from whom he was stealing. He was forced to confront the reality that crime is not just an offense against the state but against real people.[27]

The essence of restorative justice is that we are involving both the victim and the offender in the process. As Peter Walker also writes: "To view crime primarily in terms of broken relationships between people and only secondly as an offense against society's laws gives a radically different perspective on offending and on the punishment of offending behavior."[28] Walker argues that relational justice sees the relationship of the victim and offender as a pivotal one, and repairing this relationship should be a central goal of the criminal justice system.

A number of Prison Fellowship ministries around the world, including in England and Wales, have begun using a program that directly confronts the relationship between victims and offenders. Called the Sycamore Tree Project, after the story in the New Testament of Jesus' encounter with a corrupt tax collector named Zacchaeus, this program brings groups of victims into prison to meet with groups of (unrelated) offenders. Peter Walker, in a recent issue of the *Prison Service Journal*, wrote of the impact of this encounter in the lives of prisoners and victims. For example, one victim said, "Talking about the pain and the impact on our lives to those I knew had perpetrated similar crimes has really helped." Victims felt reassured, hearing burglars explain that houses are generally targeted almost spontaneously rather than after long observation or stalking. As for the offenders, some were moved to tears listening to the victims' stories, victims they were coming to know as people. One inmate charged with drug dealing at first couldn't see that he was creating any victims. In his view, "My customers wanted what I could provide. They didn't have to come to me. I wasn't forcing them to buy drugs." But by the end of the program, he could see some of the social implications of his actions. The light was dawning.[29]

I have seen how powerfully this program has worked. Last year, when I was at our InnerChange Freedom Initiative prison in Texas for a graduation service, I stood on the platform as the men came forward to receive their certificates. As one man, Ron Flowers, approached me, I saw out of the corner of my eye a tall, stately African-American woman rise to her feet and walk toward me. I knew her name—Mrs. Washington—and what was going to happen; most of the people in that room did not.

Ron Flowers had been required to attend the Sycamore Tree Project. For fourteen years in prison, Flowers had steadfastly denied his guilt. He did not even want to know the name of the mother of the woman who had been killed in the course of his crime. But one night in a Sycamore Tree session, agreeing that he needed to take some responsibility, he asked for the mother's name so that he could begin praying for her; it was Mrs. Washington. It was a small start, but as it turned out, it was a pivotal one.

One of the volunteers in the InnerChange program was Mrs. Washington's pastor. She had fought Ron's release on parole every year, and she was shocked to find out that he was in a Christian program like InnerChange. But finally she said that she wanted to meet him, that God had been speaking to her about the importance of forgiveness. For the first time in fourteen years, she found her attitude was beginning to change.

When the InnerChange staff told Ron that Mrs. Washington, the woman for whom he had started to pray, wanted to meet him, he began to weep. He confessed in tears that he had in fact shot Mrs. Washington's daughter. He was not simply the getaway driver in a robbery gone wrong.

Mrs. Washington was stunned to learn of Ron's confession and immediately agreed to meet him. It was a tearful and emotional confrontation during which Ron was able to answer many questions that had troubled Mrs. Washington all those years: Why was her daughter in that neighborhood? (A boyfriend who wanted drugs had driven her there.) Had she been involved in drugs? (No, she stayed in the car the whole time.) Why had he shot her? (He had grabbed a gun when he left his apartment; when he reached the sidewalk and saw, out of the corner of his eye, a car moving, he swung his arm around and fired once at the car, not knowing her daughter was there.) Mrs. Washington explained to Ron how this crime had affected her. Her daughter was dead. Her son became so distraught that he turned to drugs, contracted AIDS by using an infected needle, and died. Her husband suffered a stroke in the aftermath of their daughter's death, lingered for several years, and died. Mrs. Washington was now completely alone.

But both people received more than understanding. Ron, prepared by the Sycamore Tree Project, confessed what he had done, said he was very sorry, and indicated that he intended to change. Mrs. Washington, prepared by her desire to obey Scripture, forgave Ron for killing her daughter.

During the graduation, as I handed Ron Flowers his certificate, Mrs. Washington walked over and embraced him. She then turned to the crowd of volunteers, mentors, inmates, and corrections officials, announcing that Ron Flowers was now her adopted son. She had lost her daughter, her son, and her husband. She explained she had no one else, but in Christ she could now forgive and love Ron Flowers. I saw firsthand the impact of this kind of reconciliation on a room of hardened criminals and Christian workers: there were very few dry eyes in that auditorium. This is what is known as restoring *shalom*.

The story of Mrs. Washington and Ron Flowers continues to have an impact on many people. One supporter of Prison Fellowship sent a $10,000 check to Mrs. Washington as a gift. No strings attached, no tax consequences. Mrs. Washington used the money in part to help Ron Flowers make his adjustment to the outside; the balance was used to set up a scholarship fund in her daughter's honor in her church. Ron Flowers continues to meet with Mrs. Washington, usually on Sundays. She disciples him, and he has indeed become an adopted son. Only the grace of God could make this possible.

This is, of course, a dramatic illustration of what can happen when victims and offenders encounter one another. But the illustration merely reflects a growing reality in criminal justice internationally.

University of Minnesota professor Mark Umbreit, a pioneer in criminal justice, has reported that there are five hundred mediation programs and projects in Europe and more than three hundred in the United States.[30] A Canadian survey of restorative programs and projects in that country resulted in more than one hundred listings.[31] Family group conferences, another form of mediation, are used routinely in New Zealand, Australia, South Africa, the United States, and Canada. Sentencing circles, derived from Native American traditional practices, are being used in urban as well as rural settings in the United States.[32]

Many of these programs have been highly successful. Mark Umbreit conducted a study of victim-offender reconciliation programs in Albuquerque, New Mexico, and Minneapolis, Minnesota. He found that 81 percent of offenders who had participated in the face-to-face encounter programs completed their restitution agreements with their victims, compared with 58 percent fulfillment of court-ordered restitution in the nonprogram comparison groups.[33]

The New Zealand experience has been particularly significant. Under a 1989 statute, young people ages fourteen to seventeen are eligible for a family-group conference instead of a trial. The conference is attended by a variety of people: the young person and members of his or her family; the victim, often accompanied by supporters; a youth advocate or police officer or a social worker; anyone else the members of the family wish to have present; and other members of the community. The process requires the members of the group conference to agree that the crime will be punished as a result of their deliberations, thus eliminating the need for the situation to go to court. Or, if the matter has already gone to youth court, offenses admitted or proved in the court are referred to a family-group conference, which will often recommend to the court what the sanctions should be.

Three things are distinctive about this plan: (1) power is transferred from the state, principally from the court, to the community; (2) the community negotiates a response; and (3) all of those involved in the offense take part in the process, which can often lead to healing for the offender, victim, and community.

One of the results of these conferences is that the offenders accept responsibility for their crime. So often in the cold courtroom process, offenders, who must plead not guilty mainly to protect their rights, find themselves in an adversarial context, constantly trying to defend their behavior. By contrast, in the conference they are able openly to acknowledge what they have done. Victims in turn see offenders as human beings struggling with sin. The community participates and feels some responsibility not only for healing the damage that has been done but also for setting things right in the neighborhood. The New Zealand experience has been a great success.[34]

It is important to understand from this illustration that restorative justice does not tilt the scales away from individual responsibility. It may often sound as if a group conference, for example, is a therapeutic approach that diminishes the concept of an offender's being justly punished or that it could even excuse the offender's behavior. This is not the Christian view. While crime is influenced by the moral condition of a community, crime has its origins in the offender's wrong moral choices, as explained in part 3.

We need to recognize that the desire to work through relationships—to bring the Mrs. Washingtons and Ron Flowerses together—can be somewhat therapeutic. But restorative justice does not, from a Christian perspective, excuse the offender from his or her responsibility. Rather, it reflects that dialectic between the antiseptic approach and the therapeutic, and it works to maintain the balance between punishment and individual responsibility on the one hand, and reparation and healing on the other.

THE BIBLICAL DISTINCTIVE

AT THE HEART of the restorative justice model we have been discussing is the point emphasized in part 3: transformation. The key is changing the human heart, opening the way for forgiveness, reconciliation, and a new view of life.

This is why, in my experience at least, the biblical model is so effective. I do not demean secular approaches to restorative justice. Many programs offer important advances over current justice systems and, of course, can produce needed structural reforms. But at some point transformation becomes essential.

Growing numbers of restorative justice practitioners recognize this and talk about a "magic moment" in many restorative encounters in which something happens and the whole quality of the interaction changes. Many, in fact, refer to this as a spiritual moment, though unfortunately some of them look to Eastern religions or the New Age for an explanation.

The biblical view of humanity and of justice gives us the only rational explanation, one that conforms to reality, the way things really are. The biblical view not only explains sin and alienation (which no secular view does) but also offers reconciliation and the restoration of *shalom;* that is, God's ordained order. True justice is but an expression of God's character and order, when people relate to one another according to his will for the purpose of his glory. And because the image of God is in us, we should expect to be able to recognize it in ourselves and in our experiences together.

Finally, why is it we have any expectation—even hope—when we hear stories like that of Mrs. Washington and Ron Flowers? Why is reconciliation, with its relational dimensions, an alternative we find appealing? If all we wanted was security, we would long only for order. C. S. Lewis once said that when we find ourselves longing for something that we have never experienced, the most logical explanation is that we were created for something different. In my view, the desire for *shalom* is deep and exists within all people. Yet we have never experienced it in full. We have a kind of nostalgia for something we've never experienced. The Christian answer is that this is because we were created to live in *shalom*, in Eden. There is a reason the longing has not left us: Those who have come to know the Lord will one day arrive there in the new heaven and new earth. This longing is deeply imprinted in us and even in all of creation.

Christians, then, can explain not only sin and the need it raises for law but also why we long for and are able to work toward the kind of relationships that reflect, even if only for the moment, the celestial reality. There is a reality beyond ours, one to which we are invited.

TAKING BACK OUR COMMUNITIES

A 123-block area in Camden, New Jersey, does not have a single adult male living within its borders.[1] That neighborhood stands as a grotesque monument to the failed social policies discussed in part 2. What has happened in Camden, as it has happened in community after community, is that young urban males have been caught in a vicious cycle: many of them are fatherless, their consciences informed largely by a polluted popular culture; drifting through the streets in gangs, they end up arrested, in prison, on probation, parole, and back in prison. So we have literally stripped leadership out of these communities by ill-advised criminal justice and social policies.

Criminologists warn of communities reaching the "tipping point." When so many people go to prison, it destabilizes the community.[2] When the social order is so distorted, the result is more and more crime with no way to reverse the process.

I visited an area very similar to Camden. It's called Allison Hill, a section of Harrisburg, Pennsylvania, in the shadow of the state capitol and one of the worst ghettos I have ever seen. I walked the streets with the area director of Prison Fellowship. Young men were huddled in darkened doorways; alleys reeked of decaying food, old garbage, and waste from the addicts who used them as open toilets. Bullet casings and used drug needles littered the streets. Drug deals were taking place on the street, sometimes in the doorways of boarded-up buildings that were used as crack houses. Our area director showed me where the prostitutes would come out and ply their trade at night.

In the midst of this urban hell, a small storefront was rented by a local chapter of Neighbors Who Care, a Prison Fellowship subsidiary ministry that mobilizes churches to assist victims of crime. There, Neighbors Who Care teamed up with a feisty pastor named Ana Martinez of the First Spanish Christian Church. Soon the storefront office became a hubbub of activity, volunteers and victims coming in and out, offering and receiving help, and at least making a showing of Christ's concern for those suffering in this area.

Ana Martinez seized on the idea to stage a prayer march through the center of the city, much as William Booth had marched through the streets of East London a century ago. She and the Neighbors Who Care team assembled several hundred volunteers wearing bright yellow T-shirts printed with the words "When Neighbors Care, Crime Goes Down."

The group handed out hot dogs and Neighbors Who Care balloons. The chief of police came. Clowns with painted faces entertained the children. The crowds grew.

The Neighbors Who Care director noticed a neighborhood drug dealer mixing with kids, handing out balloons. She went over to the police chief: "It's a shame that the drug guy is getting involved with our kids by using our balloons," she told him. The next thing she knew, the police were taking the drug dealer away in a cruiser.

The crowd continued to swell. Soon there were five hundred people in front of the Neighbors Who Care office. From there they began the march, moving down littered streets. People held hands, sang hymns, and prayed out loud. "Shine the light," they sang. "Shine the light on Harrisburg."

As they marched on, people poured out of the local bars to see what was happening. A young woman high on drugs stumbled after them. "I need help," she sobbed, and she got it, ending up eventually in a treatment program. Kids sailing by on skateboards joined the procession.

The crowd approached a corner where a cluster of black-clad gang members were milling around, edgy with tension. Reverend Ana called out with a booming voice, "The Lord loves you. We love you. But we don't love what you're doing. Come join us."

One teenage boy, his young face already hardened from years on the streets, slowly backed away from the gang on the corner and joined the crowd of Christians.

Meanwhile carloads of teenagers gunned their motors, honking their horns and blaring their radios, trying to drown out the prayer procession. The Christians prayed even more loudly. Finally the teenagers drove away, frustrated that they could not stop the march.

Ana looked around her. Men were crying, women shaking. "The prayer was so loud," she said, "I've never heard anything like it. It was like a roar in the street, like the Israelites marching into battle for the Promised Land."

The procession continued through the city streets. Prostitutes followed along, some asking for help to escape from the pimps who controlled them. Others joined in, receiving Christ as the praying crowd moved past.

After that unforgettable night in August 1997, the Neighbors Who Care office was flooded both with victim requests for help and with people wanting to be trained as volunteers. And the work has continued as more and more citizens have taken responsibility to take back their own streets.

Just a few months ago, the governor of Pennsylvania walked through the Allison Hill area. There were no more spent bullet casings on the ground, no more hypodermic needles, no more young people slouching in darkened alleys. Allison Hill still has problems, but it is a changed place because citizens cared enough to take back their own community. They decided to restore the *shalom*.

Even kids can get in on the act. A few years ago in Montgomery, Alabama, fifty Christian teenagers armed with hedge clippers and Weedwacker trimmers descended on a neighborhood of mostly elderly people, determined to tackle the overgrown bushes that provided hiding places for vandals, burglars, and muggers. The kids trimmed towering hedges, thinned low-hanging tree branches, replaced burned-out lights, and installed peepholes in doors. The project was called Youth Cutting Down on Crime, and it was organized by Neighbors Who Care. It showed the fearful neighborhood that kids can be a force for good, not just a threat of evil.

These are but two illustrations of what is a growing movement in America today, people finally recognizing that the job of policing cannot be left to the police alone, that citizens have to reassert their responsibility for their own community and rebuild neighborhoods where people truly care for one another. As discussed in part 3, a chief contributing factor to crime is the lack of community cohesion. Researchers looking for the cause of crime by examining 382 Chicago neighborhoods found only one common denominator: It wasn't poverty or race or demographics; it was simply people not caring about their neighbors.

All these examples support the conclusions that a serious reason for the increase of crime is simply the breakdown of intermediate community structures.

Who can bring them back? Government agencies can help with their aid, to be sure. Social service groups can provide vital services. Schools can contribute. But fundamentally the only way community cohesion can be achieved is when people look beyond their narrow self-interest and care for one another.

Who can take the lead in this? Those who are commanded by their Lord to do so as an act of biblical faithfulness and obedience. This is the ripest mission field for the church, right in our own communities.

THE CHRISTIAN'S CULTURAL MANDATE

Many Christians today believe that the great task of the church is evangelism. Most of the turn-of-the-millennium conferences focused on winning the world to Christ in the next century or the next thousand years, should Christ tarry. For those of us in the evangelical tradition, evangelism has always been first and foremost on our minds. It is the *great commission*.

And in a sense, of course, that is absolutely correct. It has to be the first call on the Christian. But we often do this at the expense of a mandate that in some respects is equally crucial. This is what is called the *cultural commission* or the cultural mandate. In the Genesis account of creation, God did the work of creation directly until the sixth day. Then he turned to those he had created in his image, and he commissioned them to carry on, to have dominion, and to develop the creation. It is the work of humans as they obey God's command to be fruitful, to fill and subdue the earth.

Many Christians fail to realize that this same command is still binding on us today. Although the Fall introduced sin and evil into human history, it did not erase the cultural mandate. The generations since Adam and Eve still bear children, build families, and spread across the earth. They tend animals and plants and fields, construct cities and governments, and make music and works of art.

Sin introduced a destructive power into God's created order, but it did not obliterate that order. When we are redeemed, we are not only free from the sinful motivations that drive us, but we are also restored to begin fulfilling our original purpose, empowered to do what we were created to do.

Whenever Christians have understood that commission, they have been able to change the world around them. An instructive historical example can be found in the Dark Ages, when barbarian hordes overran Europe and devastated the art, literature, and centers of learning. But as God would have it, under the preaching of Saint Patrick, the relatively protected island of Ireland was evangelized for Jesus Christ.

Monastics began to revolutionize the world by replacing the old values of a pagan warrior society with the new values of Christianity. A culture of illiteracy became a culture of learning. The Irish monks

preserved the Scriptures and created wonderful illuminated manu-
scripts. They carefully preserved the faith, the literature, and the best
of the Greco-Roman culture.

As the barbarian hordes began to recede, the Irish monks went
forth to reevangelize Europe. They began by sending missionaries
from Ireland all across Scotland, England, and then to the Continent.
All along the way, the monks established monasteries and carried on
their tradition of copying and preserving the Bible along with every
other book they could get their hands on, including the great classics,
some of which had not been seen in Europe for centuries. They also
taught their converts Latin, music, and painting.

By early in the seventh century, nearly seven hundred monastic
communities had been established in Scotland alone. Everywhere the
Irish monks went, they carried their Bibles and books around on their
waists, just as Irish pagans had once tied their enemies' skulls to their
belts. This is "how the Irish saved civilization," to use the words of
scholar Thomas Cahill, who has written the best-selling book by that
title.[3]

For those who think that the forces of secularism are simply too
powerful today, for those who think that Christianity can work only
in its own enclaves and build its own churches, for those who think it
is impossible for Christians to redirect the culture, I suggest we go
back and read that glorious chapter in history when the Irish indeed
saved civilization and reintroduced Christianity in Europe.

We can do the same thing today. What is required? The church—
the people of God—must be the church: a community of the
redeemed, living and practicing Christian teachings. When the church
does this, it actually renews the culture around it or often creates a
culture of its own. The standards and behaviors and expectations of
people in the community are formed and established within a biblical

framework, and a society of righteousness and justice can be restored or created.

Over the past quarter century, I have seen the most dramatic demonstration of this truth in what many would consider the most unlikely places—prisons. I have been repeatedly struck by how all prisons—new and old, those in developed countries and undeveloped countries—seem to reflect the same cultural standards: There is little personal pride, and there is widespread despair and bitterness. Most prisons are dreary and dirty places, the odors often stale and foul. Cheating, lying, and profanity become a way of life. The convicts often enforce their own code of conduct, only slightly less arbitrary perhaps than the warden's rules. Con games are a way of life.

This is not to say that there are not well-run, decent prisons— there are. But even the most enlightened officials are dealing with an environment that is by its very nature oppressive and often debilitating. Prisons, after all, are populated by people who are dealing with immense personal tragedies, albeit often of their own making. Anyone who works in prison becomes accustomed to the vacant stares, the hapless prison shuffle, the anger and resentment, the constant complaints, the general social disarray.

But of the six hundred prisons I have visited in forty countries, four were memorably different. In Humaita, described earlier, the men radiated genuine joy; the chapels were full; the floors and walls were scrubbed cleaned. The common prayers before meals were spoken with firmness and conviction. Signs on the wall emphasized self-discipline and responsibility.

Humaita was run by only two staff members, supported by a team of inmate leaders. Disciplinary actions were rare. The culture inside the prison was in many respects more humane and just than the culture in the community outside the prison.

Walking into the InnerChange Freedom Initiative in Houston the first time, I was impressed by how much it felt like Humaita. The men greeted us excitedly and shared testimonies; they showed genuine pride in their prison, something I had not seen in institutions other than Humaita. The prison was spotlessly clean, and the staff seemed as enthusiastic as the inmates. Again disciplinary incidence was far lower than that of other prisons; and early reports show a dramatic drop in recidivism among those released.

The prisoner-participants, who occupy one wing of the prison, frequently hold revival services in the prison yard, bringing many inmates from the other units to Christ.

It does not take long to create this new culture. In December 1999, I attended the dedication service of the second InnerChange Freedom Initiative prison, this one in Newton, Iowa. I was not prepared for what I found. The prison had been operating only two months, and the state had placed 140 inmates with us, all at one time. It would be tough to integrate them that fast and to build much sense of community and camaraderie.

But when the gates swung open, I stepped from the cold of a dreary December day into the warm embrace of inmates alive in Christ. It was the same spirit I sensed when I had visited the Texas prison and Humaita, except these men were, if possible, even more enthusiastic. When I finished speaking in the main prison unit, the inmates clutched their Bibles in their right hand and cried out like a great festal chant, each phrase emphasized: "This is my Bible, a lamp unto my feet, a light unto my path. These words I will hide in my heart, so I may not sin against God." With each line from Psalm 119, the men would thrust their Bibles over their heads toward heaven. The sound reverberated off the concrete walls and floors. At that very moment I thought I could march those men out of that prison and assail the gates of hell.

I had not imagined it possible to take 140 inmates, many with long sentences and severe personal problems, bring them together in a new facility with a new staff, and mold them into a cohesive, joyous community. But that is precisely what I witnessed. The reports from Iowa have been as impressive as the other Prison Fellowship prisons that have been opened much longer. Such is the power of biblical truth to transform individuals and cultures alike.

Nowhere have I seen the contrast more dramatically displayed than in Quito, Ecuador, where Prison Fellowship leaders imitating Humaita took over a wing of the notorious and antiquated García Moreno Prison. In 1996 I took a delegation of corrections officials to visit the prison. There were fresh bloodstains on the steps of the entranceway as we passed through, the result of someone having been beaten while he was dragged into the prison. We then toured the infamous punishment cells that had once been torture chambers, buried deep in the old stone-and-cement structure. Darkened cubicles, illuminated only by shafts of light from small grates at the top of the walls, now housed twelve inmates. But with only four bunks, the inmates had to sleep in shifts. There was no running water; the floors were covered with grime.

When we left those cells, we were taken to view the central compound, where more than four hundred inmates were milling about. Through a barred iron gate we gazed in disbelief into the courtyard. The scene before us was something out of a Dickens novel: hundreds of men shuffling around the yard, many dressed in rags, and all of them wearing vacant expressions of hopelessness on their pale, drawn faces. A group of garishly made-up women huddled together against one of the side walls.

We asked if we could go into the yard, and after some initial resistance the officials allowed us to, although I noticed that no guards accompanied us. Standing in the center of that compound, we began to speak. Men came from all quarters, including "their women" who turned out to be transvestites. Several men were limping; a man with only one leg was helped by another prisoner. Standing directly in front of me was a man with an empty eye socket, open sores covering his face. Several men had scarves covering their faces, perhaps to cover sores or to filter the vile smells.

These were among the most wretched souls I have met in any prison anywhere. The conditions in the prison were unspeakably bad, and corruption was pervasive. Jorge Crespo, a distinguished citizen in Ecuador and the chairman of our Prison Fellowship ministry there, led us out of the compound through another darkened corridor into Pavilion C, the unit that was turned over to our ministry. As Crespo swung open the gates, it was like walking from darkness into a radiant light. At the far end of the cellblock was what looked like an altar with a huge cross silhouetted against a brightly painted concrete wall. Gathered in the open area before the altar were more than two hundred inmates singing, applauding, many playing guitars. They were glowing with joy and enthusiasm. Within seconds we were surrounded, and the prisoners began embracing us like long-separated brothers.

But Pavilion C was only the beginning. Crespo proudly escorted us into Casa de San Pablo, a wing that had been turned into a spotlessly clean living area. Men had built bunks, decorating the area to make it feel like home. In fact, the inmates called the institution "the Home." The chapel was packed with men who had graduated into this unit; they had jobs on the outside and had been matched with mentors. There in the Home I participated in one of the most joyous worship services I've been in anywhere else in the world.

This one institution housed programs that represented two separate worlds. One program, separated from the other by perhaps a hundred feet, was full of darkness, despair, hopelessness, and perversion; the other was full of light, hope, joy, and community. What made the difference? Simply the presence of Christian people who were living out their faith in the midst of some of the most deprived and desperate human beings to be found anywhere on planet Earth.

Admittedly, reforming or creating a new culture in a huge, diverse society is a different and in some ways a more daunting task than creating one in a controlled environment of a prison. But there are distinct parallels and certainly lessons to be learned. Society is changed, after all, one person at a time, one neighborhood at a time, one city at a time.

Humaita and her progeny proved to us that it is possible, that the biblical model can produce a just and righteous community. They prove that *shalom* can be restored even under the most desperate circumstances of what otherwise would be forlorn and hopeless places called prison.

CONCLUSION

The Christian church can indeed be an influence in renewing culture. And where is there a more important place to start than in providing modern society with an answer to the foundational questions such as, What is justice? How do we create a society that preserves order and maximizes liberty, one that creates the peace and harmony that Christians and Jews know as the *shalom*?

As I hope has become clear, only a biblical view of justice enables society to accomplish this. First, only the biblical view establishes a transcendent authority for the law that enables people to live in security under a rule of law, which is objectively true. Without this, we fall into moral nihilism or tyranny.

Second, the biblical view recognizes the reality of sin and thus provides a mechanism to restrain it. Utopianism—the idea that people are good and can be made better—has proven itself to be not only a false philosophy but also a dangerous one indeed.

Third, the biblical worldview provides the only way out of the human dilemma. We may think we're good, but how do we account for the wrong that we do? And once we do it, how do we deal with the guilt? Is there any way to be redeemed? Only the biblical worldview provides a way for the human heart to be transformed and for the problem of crime to be identified and dealt with.

Finally, a Christian worldview provides a motivation and a blueprint for restoring communities and relationships that have been ravaged by crime. The power of God made manifest through his people and his Word provides the essential impetus for loving one's neighbor and indeed one's enemy and forgiving our transgressions against one another. The Christian worldview stands alone as the hope for the realization of true justice, and there has not been a more propitious movement in modern times in which to present this Christian answer to the question, What is justice?

You see, modern men and women have emerged from a century that will be well remembered for its ideological domination and grand, sweeping utopian promises. Think of the parade of "isms" that stirred the fevered passions of twentieth-century intellectuals. The century began with the hubris of post-Edwardian triumphalism and the promises of Darwin and Hegel. Progress, they assured us, would inevitably evolve from expanded knowledge. Then there were Dewey and Freud, promising that we could find the good within ourselves if only we threw off our guilt, neuroses, and cultural repression. Then came the domination of scientism and naturalism, which assured us that modern enlightenment could take God's place and do a far better job. Marxism burst on the scene in its various incarnations, promising to deliver us from repressing economic and cultural forces. Then came national socialism. And humanism. And existentialism.

But all have proven to be bankrupt—or, worse, an excuse for

unspeakable evil. As I remarked earlier, utopianism always paves the way for tyranny.

The most beguiling promise of all was advanced in the 1960s: God is dead, so we live to overcome the nothingness with free expression and heroic individualism. Personal autonomy became the Holy Grail, the ultimate object of life. But the passion for autonomy skewed our laws and shattered our cultural taboos, resulting in an untenable moral nihilism. Today people are finally discovering that they cannot live with the logical conclusions of the worldview they so enthusiastically embraced in the latter half of the twentieth century. So in increasing numbers, people are searching for something better. Thus it is that the old questions, the timeless ones, are being asked again, questions as basic as these: What is justice? Can we create a just and moral framework by which to order our common lives together?

There is an answer to these insistent questions. It is a view of justice that acknowledges the created moral order and thereby preserves the peaceful order with minimum infringement of human liberty, what the American Founders referred to as ordered liberty. Central to achieving this, however, is a criminal justice system that not only provides just deserts, but provides redemption as well, one that restores the *shalom* of the community shattered by crime.

This, then, is the opportunity of this moment in history. After decades of expensive failures in corrections in criminal justice, the time is at hand to turn to what may seem a new and radical model but is actually an old and well-proven one: justice that restores.

NOTES

Introduction

1. Charles Colson and Nancy Pearcey, *How Now Shall We Live?* (Wheaton, Ill.: Tyndale House, 1999).
2. Some of the material in this book was prepared for the London Lectures, a series sponsored by John Stott and the London Institute of Contemporary Christianity. Those lectures, with their British focus, have been preserved in *Justice That Restores* (Leicester, England: InterVarsity Press, 2000).

Chapter 1: Crisis in Criminal Justice

1. Bill Broadway, "A Higher Calling Against Guns? Accosted Priests' Different Fates Move Self-Defense Debate Beyond Bible Verses," *Washington Post*, 15 June 2000.
2. Michael Satchell, Dorian Friedman, and Lee Neville, "Crying Wolf—Whale, That Is, Holy Wail," *U.S. News & World Report* (May 4, 1998): 14.
3. Allen J. Beck and Christopher J. Mumola, "Prisoners in 1998," in *Bureau of Justice Statistics Bulletin,* U.S. Department of Justice, August 1999.
4. Mike Maguire, "Crime Statistics, Patterns, and Trends," in *The Oxford Handbook of Criminology*, 2d ed., ed. Mike Maguire, Rodney Morgan, and Robert Reiner (Oxford, England: Clarendon Press, 1997): 158.
5. Callie Marie Rennison, "Criminal Victimization 1998: Changes 1997–98 with Trends 1993–98," in *Bureau of Justice Statistics Bulletin,* U.S. Department of Justice, July 1999. (This is based on National Crime Victimization Survey data.)
6. Arrests reported to the FBI, "Crime in the U.S." *Uniform Crime Report Program, 1960 and 1980.* Howard N. Snyder, "Juvenile Arrests 1997," in *Juvenile Justice Bulletin,* U.S. Department of Justice, Office of Juvenile Justice and Delinquency Programs. On-line (http://www.ojjdp.ncjrs.org/jjbulletin/9812_2/intro.html), December 1998.
7. Howard N. Snyder, "Murders Known to Involve Juvenile Offenders, 1980–1995," in *U.S. Department of Justice, Office of Juvenile Justice and Delinquency Prevention Statistical Briefing Book.* On-line (http://www.ojjdp.ncjrs.org/ojstatbb/qa051.html), September 1998.
8. Diane Weathers, "Stop the Guns," *Essence* (December 1993): 67.
9. Ibid.
10. John DiIulio, "The Coming of the Super-Predators," *Weekly Standard,* 27 November 1995.
11. Shay Bilchik, "1997 National Youth Gang Survey," *U.S. Department of Justice, Office of Juvenile Justice and Delinquency Prevention.*
12. Rogers Worthington, "Jury Rejects Girl's Defense of Insanity Due to Hard Life," *Houston Chronicle,* 8 November 1992.
13. Bill Bryan and Kim Bell, "More Teens, More Guns Equal More Deaths, Experts Say," *St. Louis Post-Dispatch,* 29 August 1993.

14. Stephen Braun, "Boy, 5, Killed for Refusing to Steal Candy, Cops Say Other Kids, 10 & 11, Drop Him from 14th-Floor Apartment," *The Record*, 15 October 1994.
15. Robert Hanley, "Older Suspect in Pizza Killings Was Mastermind, Officials Say," *New York Times*, 23 April 1997.
16. Patricia Hurtado, "Chilling Words/Statements Relate Teen's Account of Central Park Killings," *Newsday* (October 4, 1997): 13.
17. Laurie Goodstein and Blaine Hardin, "Of Birth, Death, and the Prom," *Washington Post*, 10 June 1997.
18. Maria Eftimiades et al., "Why Are Kids Killing?" *People* (June 23, 1997): 46.
19. Snyder, "Murders Known to Involve Juvenile Offenders, 1980–1995."
20. C. S. Lewis, "Men without Chests," in *The Abolition of Man* (New York: Touchstone Books, 1975), 27.
21. David Grossman and Mary Cagney, "Trained to Kill; Children Who Kill," *Christianity Today* (August 10, 1998): 31.

Chapter 2: The Fundamental Basis of Justice and the Law

1. William Blackstone, *Commentaries on the Laws of England*, vol. 1 (Chicago: University of Chicago Press, 1979), 41.
2. Daniel Ritchie, ed., *Edmund Burke: Appraisals and Applications* (New Brunswick, N.J.: Transaction Publishers, 1991), 222.
3. Allan Bloom, *The Closing of the American Mind: How Higher Education Has Failed Democracy and Impoverished the Souls of Today's Students* (New York: Simon & Schuster, 1987), 25.
4. Arthur Schlesinger, *Brown Alumni Monthly* (May 1989): 18, 22.
5. George Barna, *What Americans Believe: An Annual Survey of Values and Religious Views in the United States* (Ventura, Calif.: Regal, 1991), 84.
6. Ibid., 170.
7. George Gallup, "Few Believe in Moral Absolutes, but Most Want to Follow God's Teachings," *PRRC Emerging Trends* (February 1989): 9–16.

Chapter 3: The Consequences of the Rise of Naturalism

1. C. S. Lewis, "Men without Chests," in *The Abolition of Man* (New York: Touchstone Books, 1975), 15.
2. *Romer v. Evans*, 517 US 620 (1996).
3. *Planned Parenthood v. Casey*, 505 US 833 (1992).
4. Michael Sandel, *Democracy's Discontent: America in Search of a Public Philosophy* (Cambridge, Mass.: Harvard University Press, 1996).
5. C. S. Lewis, "The Poison of Subjectivism," *Christian Reflections* (Grand Rapids: Eerdmans, 1994), 75.
6. Ibid., 81.

Chapter 4: The Implications for Criminal Justice

1. Ted Oliver, "H-block Slams Door on Grim History," *Sunday Telegraph*, 23 July 2000.

2. Jonathan Burnside, "Justice, Seriousness, and Relationships," *Law and Relationism,* ed. Paul R. Beaumont (Carlisle, England: Paternoster, 2000), passim.

Chapter 5: Deprivation or Depravity?

1. Edward T. Oakes, "Original Sin: A Disputation," *First Things* (November 1998): 21.
2. John Henry Newman, *Apologia Pro Vita Sua,* quoted in Oakes, "Original Sin," 20.
3. Jean-Jacques Rousseau, *The Social Contract* (Boston: Charles E. Tuttle, Everyman's Classic Library, 1993), 181.
4. Denis Diderot, quoted in Gertrude Himmelfarb, *One Nation, Two Cultures: A Searching Examination of American Society in the Aftermath of Our Cultural Revolution* (New York: Alfred A. Knopf, 1999), 111.
5. David Lamb, "Shadow on Sunset Years in Cambodia," *Los Angeles Times,* 20 May 1999.
6. Anatole France, quoted in Oakes, "Original Sin: A Disputation," 16.
7. C. S. Lewis, "The Humanitarian Theory of Punishment," in *God in the Dock* (Grand Rapids: Eerdmans, 1970), 287.
8. Clarence Darrow, *Attorney for the Damned,* ed. Arthur Weinberg (New York: Simon & Schuster, 1957), 3–4.
9. Jimmy Carter, in an interview with the National Black Network, Weekly Compilation of Presidential Documents, July 1977.
10. Ramsey Clark, *Crime in America: Observations on Its Nature, Causes, Prevention, and Control* (New York: Simon & Schuster, 1970), 17–18.
11. The National Advisory Commission on Criminal Justice Standards and Goals, 1973, quoted in Gerald Austin McHugh, *Christian Faith in Criminal Justice: Toward a Christian Response to Crime and Punishment* (New York: Paulist Press, 1978), 66–67.
12. M. MacGuigan, "Report to Parliament by the Subcommittee on the Penitentiary System in Canada" (Ottawa, Canada: Ministry of Supply and Services, 1977), 35.
13. James O. Finckenauer and Patricia W. Gavin, *Scared Straight: The Panacea Phenomenon Revisited* (Prospect Heights, Ill.: Waveland Press, 1999).
14. James Q. Wilson, "What to Do about Crime," *Commentary* (September 1994): 26.
15. U.S. Department of Justice, "Prisoners in State and Federal Institutions (1971–1977)," quoted in *Sourcebook of Criminal Justice Statistics—1979,* ed. Timothy Flanagan, Michael Hindelang, and Michael Gottfredson (Albany, N.Y.: Criminal Justice Research Center, 1980), 633.
16. *The 1997 Corrections Yearbook* (New York: Criminal Justice Institute, 1998) reported U.S. correctional budgets totaling $28.9 billion and anticipated a 4.8 percent growth for the following year.
17. Eric Schlosser, "The Prison-Industrial Complex," *Atlantic Monthly* (December 1998): 52.
18. Leon Dash and Susan Sheehan, "Justice System Catches Up with Brothers in Crime," *Washington Post,* 30 November 1998.
19. William Temple, *The Ethics of Penal Action* (London: The Clarke Hall Fellowship, 1934), 40, quoted in *Relational Justice: Repairing the Breach,* eds. Jonathan Burnside and Nicola Baker (Winchester, England: Waterside Press, 1994), 139.

Chapter 6: The Consequences of Utopian Notions of Criminal Justice

1. John Leo, "The It's-Not-My-Fault Syndrome," *U.S. News & World Report* 108, no. 24 (June 18, 1990): 16.
2. Mona Charen, "Blame It on My Hormones, Not the Booze," *Newsday* (June 12, 1991).
3. George F. Will, "Shocking Crimes, Astounding Sentences," *Washington Post*, 11 December 1983.
4. George Flynn, "Woman Sues Houston Nightclub over Hot-Dog Eating Contest," *Houston Chronicle*, 25 March 1997.
5. C. S. Lewis, "The Humanitarian Theory of Punishment," in *God in the Dock* (Grand Rapids: Eerdmans, 1970), 292.
6. Ibid.
7. Ibid.

Chapter 7: A Realistic View of Human Nature

1. Mini Hall, "Clinton Sings Praises of Teen Curfew," *USA Today*, 31 May 1996.
2. Ana Menendez and April Witt, "Most Are Ready to Pay to Get Tough on Crime," *Miami Herald*, 15 November 1993.
3. Larry Rother, "National Guard Joins Puerto Rico Police on Beat as Crime Rises," *New York Times*, 28 July 1993.
4. Fred Barbash, "Alarmed by Crime Surge, Britain Narrows Rights," *Washington Post*, 11 November 1994, 1.
5. "Partners in Crime: The Threat to British Liberty," *The Economist* (February 15, 1997): 15.

Chapter 8: The Moral Roots of Crime

1. Christie Davies, "Crime and the Rise and Decline of a Relational Society," in *Relational Justice: Repairing the Breach,* eds. Jonathan Burnside and Nicola Baker (Winchester, England: Waterside Press, 1994), 31.
2. Augustine, *Confessions,* book 2, chapter 3.
3. Samuel Yochelson and Stanton E. Samenow, *The Criminal Personality: A Profile for Change*, vol. 1 (New York: Jason Aronson, 1982), 19–20, 36.
4. James Q. Wilson and Richard J. Herrnstein, *Crime and Human Nature* (New York: Simon & Schuster, 1986), 491.
5. Davies, "Crime and the Rise and Decline of a Relational Society," 31.
6. Wilson and Herrnstein, *Crime and Human Nature,* 435.
7. Michael Schluter and David Lee, *The R Factor* (London: Hodder & Stoughton, 1993).
8. Paul Johnson, *Modern Times: The World from the Twenties to the Eighties* (New York: Harper & Row, 1983), 246–47.
9. J. Edwin Orr, *The Flaming Tongue: The Impact of Twentieth Century Revivals* (Chicago: Moody Press, 1973), 17–18.
10. Michael Novak, "The Causes of Virtue" (speech given in Washington, D.C., January 31, 1994, reprinted by Prison Fellowship in *Sources,* no. 6 [1994]).

Chapter 9: The Moral Answer

1. Jennifer Harper, " 'Sacred' Ad Texts Strike Some as Profane: Religious Critics Hit Auto, Toilet Pitches," *Washington Times*, 12 November 1997.
2. C. S. Lewis, "Men without Chests," in *The Abolition of Man* (New York: Touchstone, 1996), 35.
3. Byron R. Johnson, David B. Larson, and Timothy C. Pitts, "Religious Programs, Institutional Adjustment, and Recidivism among Former Inmates in Prison Fellowship Programs," *Justice Quarterly* 14, no. 1 (March 1997), 145–66.
4. Amy Ridenour, "Be Thankful for Dads," *National Policy Analysis,* no. 252 (June 1999).
5. Kevin N. Wright and Karen E. Wright, *Family Life, Delinquency, and Crime: A Policymaker's Guide* (Washington, D.C.: U.S. Department of Justice, Office of Juvenile Justice and Delinquency Prevention, 1995).
6. Barbara Dafoe Whitehead, "Dan Quayle Was Right," *Atlantic Monthly* 271, no. 4 (April 1993): 47.
7. Michael McManus, "Voters Should Care about Divorce Reform," *Detroit News*, 19 September 1996.
8. "Boys with Absentee Dads Twice as Likely to Be Jailed: Stepfathers Don't Help, Study Finds," *Washington Post*, 21 August 1998.
9. Whitehead, "Dan Quayle Was Right," 47.
10. *Boy Scouts of America* et al. *v. Dale,* 99 US 699 (2000).
11. John J. DiIulio, "Broken Bottles: Liquor, Disorder, and Crime in Wisconsin," *Wisconsin Policy Research Institute Report* 8, no. 4 (May 1995).
12. Delores Kong, "Study Shows Cohesiveness Curbs Neighborhood Violence," *Boston Globe*, 15 August 1997.

Chapter 10: Christianity's Role in Transformation

1. Michael Novak, "The Causes of Virtue" (speech given in Washington, D.C., January 31, 1994, reprinted by Prison Fellowship in *Sources,* no. 6 [1994]).

Chapter 11: Restorative Justice

1. Albert Eglash, "Beyond Restitution: Creative Restitution," in *Restitution in Criminal Justice,* ed. Joe Hudson and Burt Galaway (Lexington, Mass.: D. C. Heath, 1977), 91–92.
2. Daniel Van Ness and Karen Strong, *Restoring Justice* (Cincinnati, Ohio: Anderson Publishing, 1997), 41.
3. Jonathan Burnside and Nicola Baker, eds., *Relational Justice: Repairing the Breach* (Winchester, England: Waterside Press, 1994), 131.
4. Ibid., 45.
5. Daniel W. Van Ness, *Crime and Its Victims: What We Can Do* (Downers Grove, Ill.: InterVarsity Press, 1986), 117–18.
6. William Wilberforce, quoted in Garth Lean, *God's Politician: William Wilberforce's Struggle* (London: Darton, Longman, & Todd, 1980), 74.
7. Eric Monkkone, *Police in Urban America: 1860–1920* (Cambridge, England: Cambridge

University Press, 1981), quoted in Fred Siegel, *The Future Once Happened Here* (New York: The Free Press, 1997), 192.

8. James Q. Wilson and George L. Kelling, "Broken Windows: The Police and Neighborhood Safety," *Atlantic Monthly* (March 1982): 29.

9. John Carlin, "How They Cleaned Up Precinct 75," *The Independent*, 7 January 1996.

10. "Symposium: Three Days of Hope," *Pennsylvania Gazette* (January–February 1999): 12–13.

11. Saint Augustine, *The City of God*, trans. Marcus Dods (New York: Modern Library, 1950), 690. In the Middle Ages, Thomas Aquinas gave Augustine's insight a more positive interpretation, arguing that the state is not only a remedial institution established to curb sin but that it is also a good thing in itself, an expression of our social nature. Living within social institutions is essential to fulfilling our own nature.

Chapter 12: Elements of Restorative Justice

1. Nora Greenaway, " 'Mad-as-Hell' U.S. Police Chief Scares Off Dealers' Customers," *Ottawa Citizen*, 23 February 1992.

2. Christopher Compston, "Local Justice: A Personal View," in *Relational Justice: Repairing the Breach,* eds. Jonathan Burnside and Nicola Baker (Winchester, England: Waterside Press, 1994), 83.

3. Center for Court Innovation. On-line <http://www.courtinnovation.org/demo_09rhcjc.html>

4. Jill Smolowe, "Going Soft on Crime," *Time* (November 14, 1994): 63.

5. John DiIulio, "Two Million Prisoners Are Enough," *Wall Street Journal*, 12 March 1999.

6. Tony's story was faxed from Choice, December 1994. Choice is a program of the University of Maryland, Baltimore Campus, Shriver Center. On-line <http://www.shrivercenter.org/service>

7. James Q. Wilson, "Crime and Public Policy," in *Crime,* ed. James Q. Wilson and Joan Petersilia (San Francisco: ICS Press, 1995), 504.

8. Deann Alford, "Bush's Faith-Based Plans," *Christianity Today* (October 25, 1999): 20.

9. Tim Stafford, "The Criminologist Who Discovered Churches," *Christianity Today* (June 14, 1999): 34.

10. Jack Maple, "Police Must Be Held Accountable," *Newsweek* (June 21, 1999): 67.

11. DiIulio, "Two Million Prisoners Are Enough."

12. Ellen Anderson and Charlie Weaver, "Put Money into Prevention Programs Not More Prisons," *Minnesota Star Tribune,* 8 March 1995.

13. William Edgars and John O'Leary, "The Beat Generation," *Policy Review* (Fall 1995): 4.

14. Thomas Bonczar and Allen J. Beck, "Lifetime Likelihood of Going to State or Federal Prison," *Bureau of Justice Statistics Special Report,* U.S. Department of Justice, March 1997.

15. "Facts about Prisons and Prisoners," *The Sentencing Project*, March 1999. On-line <http://www.sentencingproject.org/pubs/tsppubs/1035bs.html>

16. Timothy Egan, "The War on Crack Retreats," *New York Times*, 28 February 1999.

17. Ibid.

18. James Q. Wilson, "What to Do about Crime," *Commentary Magazine* (September 1994): 25.
19. Egan, "The War on Crack Retreats."
20. John DiIulio, "Against Mandatory Minimums," *National Review*, 17 May 1999.
21. Fyodor Dostoyevsky, quoted in Joseph Frank, *Dostoyevsky: Years of Ordeal* (Princeton, N.J.: Princeton University Press, 1983), 159.
22. Jack Eckerd and Charles Colson, *Why America Doesn't Work* (Dallas: Word, 1991), xi.
23. Sir David Ramsbotham, "The Healthy Prison, a Question of Relationships," *Relational Justice Bulletin*, 3 (1999).
24. Florida Department of Corrections Bureau of Research and Data Analysis, Community Supervision Section, "Community Control/Electronic Monitoring Admissions from July 1, 1993, to June 30, 1999—Outcomes as of June 30, 1999."
25. Based on a sermon delivered by Tony Evans at Oak Cliff Bible Fellowship, Dallas, Texas, April 10, 1994.
26. Kenneth A. Breivik, "The Importance of Restitution," *South Carolina Justice Fellowship Report,* January 1999.
27. Peter Walker, "Repairing the Breach: A Personal Motivation," in *Relational Justice: Repairing the Breach*, eds. Jonathan Burnside and Nicola Baker (Winchester, England: Waterside Press, 1994), 148.
28. Ibid.
29. Peter Walker, "Saying Sorry, Acting Sorry: The Sycamore Tree Project, a Model for Restorative Justice in Prison," *Prison Service Journal* 123 (May 1999): 19–20.
30. Mark S. Umbreit, "Victim-Offender Mediation" (paper presented at Hamline University School of Law Symposium "Restorative Justice and the Religious Traditions," Minneapolis, Minnesota, October 1998).
31. Jane Miller-Ashton and Jan Turner, "Events and Initiatives related to Restorative Justice (Recent and Upcoming)," Correctional Service of Canada and Saskatchewan Justice, September 1997.
32. Elmar G. M. Weitekamp, "Research on Victim-Offender Mediation: Findings and Needs for the Future" (paper presented at the First Conference of the European Forum for Victim-Offender Mediation and Restorative Justice, Leuven, Belgium, October 27–29, 1999).
33. Mark S. Umbreit, *Victim Meets Offender: The Impact of Restorative Justice and Mediation* (Monsey, N.Y.: Willow Tree Press, 1994), 112.
34. Fred McElrea, "Justice in the Community: The New Zealand Experience," in *Relational Justice: Repairing the Breach*, eds. Jonathan Burnside and Nicola Baker (Winchester, England: Waterside Press, 1994), 193.

Chapter 13: The Biblical Distinctive

1. Wayne R. Bryant, "New Jersey's Welfare Overhaul," *Washington Post*, 1 October 1995.
2. Michael Fletcher, "High Imprisonment Rates Could Fuel Crime," *Washington Post*, 12 July 1999.
3. Thomas Cahill, *How the Irish Saved Civilization* (New York: Doubleday, 1995).

With Gratitude

1. Daniel Van Ness, *Crime and Its Victims* (Downers Grove, Ill.: InterVarsity Press, 1986); Daniel Van Ness and Charles Colson, *Convicted: New Hope for Ending America's Crime Crisis* (Westchester, Ill.: Crossway, 1989); Daniel Van Ness and Karen Heetderks Strong, *Restoring Justice* (Cincinnati: Anderson Publishing, 1997).
2. Jonathan Burnside and Nicola Baker, eds., *Relational Justice: Repairing the Breach* (Winchester, England: Waterside Press, 1994).

WITH GRATITUDE

I HAVE BEEN substantially assisted in this project by a number of friends and colleagues to whom I am greatly indebted:

David Wagner, professor at Regent University Law School, who worked with me not only in formulating these arguments but also in preparing this manuscript.

Evelyn Bence, a long-time colleague at Prison Fellowship, who put her great editing skills to work in converting lectures to text. Evelyn is every writer's dream, a friendly and congenial editor.

My colleagues Karen Heetderks Strong and Daniel Van Ness. Karen, who is vice president of the Research and Development Division of Prison Fellowship Ministries (U.S.A.), is an extraordinarily gifted thinker with a deep understanding of restorative justice. Karen's help throughout this process was invaluable. Dan is the founding president of Justice Fellowship, now vice president of Prison Fellowship International. At the risk of being slightly expansive, I doubt that any other person, anywhere, knows more about restorative justice than Dan does. His review of the material presented here was an enormous help to me. I should note that Karen and Dan pioneered many of the ideas presented in this book. If you wish to dig a bit deeper into the area of criminal justice, I recommend three books for further study: *Crime and Its Victims* (Dan), *Convicted* (a book I coauthored with Dan), and *Restoring Justice* (Dan and Karen).[1]

I am grateful to my friend and counselor T. M. Moore, who provided able theological and substantial policy review, and to my research assistant, Kim Robbins, for her skillful management of the editorial and research process.

And I have drawn heavily on the work of Jonathan Burnside, who is himself a pioneer in what the Bristish call relational justice, similar to much of what we call restorative justice. Jonathan works with the Relationships Foundation, located in Cambridge, England. I enthusiastically commend their work, including a superb book entitled *Relational Justice: Repairing the Breach,* which gives an irresistible case for relational or restorative justice.[2]

I also want to express my appreciation to Ken Petersen, acquisitions director at Tyndale House, whose support and keen interest in communicating this message has been an encouragement to me. Many thanks to Lynn Vanderzalm, the Tyndale editor who has worked with me on this and other projects. Lynn has skillfully edited the London Lectures for an American audience.

ABOUT THE AUTHOR

CHARLES W. COLSON graduated with honors from Brown University and received his Juris Doctor from George Washington University. From 1969 to 1973 he served as special counsel to President Richard Nixon. In 1974 he pleaded guilty to charges related to Watergate and served seven months in a federal prison.

Before going to prison, Charles Colson was converted to Christ, as told in *Born Again*. He has also published *Life Sentence, Crime and the Responsible Community, Convicted* (with Dan Van Ness), *How Now Shall We Live?* (with Nancy Pearcey), *The Body* (with Ellen Vaughn), *A Dance with Deception* (with Nancy Pearcey), *A Dangerous Grace* (with Nancy Pearcey), *Gideon's Torch* (with Ellen Vaughn), *Burden of Truth* (with Anne Morse), *The God of Stones and Spiders, Why America Doesn't Work* (with Jack Eckerd), *Answers to Your Kids' Questions* (with Harold Fickett), *Who Speaks for God?, Kingdoms in Conflict, Against the Night,* and *Loving God,* the book many people consider to be a contemporary classic.

Colson founded Prison Fellowship Ministries (PF), an interdenominational outreach, now active in eighty-eight countries. The world's largest prison ministry, PF manages over 50,000 active volunteers in the U.S. and tens of thousands more abroad. The ministry provides Bible studies in more than 1,000 prisons, conducts over 2,000 in-prison seminars per year, does major evangelistic outreaches, and reaches more than 500,000 kids at Christmas with gifts and the love of Christ. The ministry also has two subsidiaries: Justice Fellowship, which works for biblically based criminal justice policies, and Neighbors Who Care, a network of volunteers providing assistance to victims of crime. Also a part of the ministry is the Wilberforce Forum, which provides worldview materials for the Christian community, including Colson's daily radio broadcast, *BreakPoint,* now heard on a thousand outlets.

Colson has received fifteen honorary doctorates and in 1993 was awarded the Templeton Prize, the world's largest cash gift (over $1 million), which is given each year to the one person in the world who has done the most to advance the cause of religion. Colson donated this prize, as he does all speaking fees and royalties, to further the work of PF.

WHAT PEOPLE ARE SAYING ABOUT
HOW NOW SHALL WE LIVE?

"A bracing challenge—just what the Christian church needs to hear in the new millenium. A very powerful book."

The Honorable Jack Kemp

"How Now Shall We Live? is truly inspiring for those who want to restore to our culture the values that made America great. It reminds us that we must not only defend what we believe, but also inspire others to give witness to the truth alongside us."

The Honorable Tom DeLay, Majority Whip, United States House of Representatives

"The singular pleasure that comes from it is its absolute—learned—refusal to give any quarter to the dogged materialists who deny any possibility that there was a creator around the corner. This is a substantial book, but the reader never tires, as one might from a catechistic marathon. The arguments are cogently and readably presented."

William F. Buckley in National Review

"The newest—and certainly the most important—of Charles Colson's books . . . the essence of this book is that the Christian faith is not just a theory, not just a system, not just a framework. It is an all-consuming way of life, robustly applicable to every minute of every day of the rest of your life."

World

"There is something wrong with the historical development of the evangelical mind, . . . a lopsidedness, a prodigious development of one divine gift coupled with the atrophy of another. . . . We know a great deal about saving grace, but next to nothing—though it is one of our doctrines—about common grace. The ambition of Charles

Colson and Nancy Pearcey is to do something about this lopsidedness, to strike a blow against the scandal of the evangelical
mind. . . . A highly intelligent book, it is not ashamed to speak to
ordinary folk."
First Things

"How Now Shall We Live? is brilliantly lit by its in-depth and succinct
diagnosis of the modern mentality . . . an intelligent and thorough-
going critique from a Scriptural perspective, of the American/
Western culture. . . . The book is a veritable mosaic of precious intellectual gems, artistically designed by Charles Colson and Nancy
Pearcey. . . . This book is a virtual 'must' for the thinking Orthodox
reader."
DOXA, a quarterly review serving the Orthodox Church

"A magnum opus in the best Schaefferian tradition. It is clearly
intended to be . . . a handbook for today's Christian. . . . The authors
presuppose that Christianity is more than just a religion of personal
salvation: it involves a total world-and-life view."
Christianity Today

"A very good and much needed book. . . . Colson argues that
Christianity isn't a private faith but a public worldview that, for
believers, permeates politics, the arts, education, science and
culture."
Insight

An "elegantly written tutorial on adopting a biblical worldview and
the discipline of thinking Christianly."
Good News

"I'd like to recommend a book. It's *How Now Shall We Live?* by
Charles Colson, the Watergate guy who got religion while in
prison. . . . Now I don't agree with everything Colson says, but the
importance of the book is that it raises a question every American
ought to face and then answer to his or her own satisfaction: What
is your world view?"
Charley Reese, nationally syndicated columnist

One of "Ten Books Every Preacher Should Read This Year."
Preaching

"Deeply troubled by the lack of biblical literacy within the American Church, this is Colson's heroic effort to enable believers to accept the importance of having a biblical worldview and devoting themselves to adopting such a life perspective. . . . This book provides a wealth of insight into how we may effectively challenge the post-Christian, post-modern culture in which we live." **The Barna Report**

"Colson and Pearcey aren't talking about influencing business, politics and culture—they want it transformed through a coherent Christian world view. Their book will challenge every Christian leader to make an honest assessment about his or her commitment to use leadership gifts in the new millennium to the cause of Christ."
Christian Management Report

"Colson and Pearcey challenge the church to stay on the front lines. Believing that America is on the verge of a great spiritual breakthrough, the authors want to equip readers to show the world that Christianity is a life system that *works* in every area—family relationships, education, science, and popular culture." **Virtue**

"A radical challenge to all Christians to understand biblical faith as an entire world view, a perspective on all of life. Through inspiring teaching and true stories, Colson discusses how to expose the false views and values of modern culture, how to live more fulfilling and satisfying lives in line with the way God created us to live—and more." **Youthworker**

[In developing and implementing an organizational learning strategy and integrating it with their organizational practices] "When it came to selecting materials, your *How Now Shall We Live?* was at the top of the list. To our minds this is now the best introduction to a Christian worldview and Christian cultural engagement available in English. At least in our organization, *How Now Shall We Live?* should become an indispensable resource."
Christian Labour Association of Canada
1999 Books of the Year—Award of Merit—Christianity Today

175

How Now Shall We Live? helps Christians make sense of the competing worldviews that clamor for attention and allegiance in a pluralistic society. Pulling no punches, Colson and Pearcey show that all other worldviews fail to meet the test of rational consistency or practical application in the real world. Only the Christian worldview provides a rationally sustainable way to understand the universe. Only the Christian worldview fits the real world and can be lived out consistently in every area of life.

Weaving together engaging stories with penetrating analysis of ideas, *How Now Shall We Live?* helps Christians defend their faith and live out its full implications in every arena—the home, workplace, classroom, courtroom, and public policy. It is a defining book for Christians in the next millennium.

Resources available from Tyndale House Publishers that support the message and ministry of *How Now Shall We Live?*

How Now Shall We Live? cloth

How Now Shall We Live? Study Guide: paper
Two sixteen-week lessons to help Bible study groups absorb and apply the concepts of Colson's magnum opus

How Now Shall We Live? Audio Book:
The abridged version on four audio cassettes

Answers to Your Kids' Questions
A guide to help parents know how to talk to their kids
about the worldview issues they face every day

Complete adult and youth video curriculum is available from LifeWay
Church Resources.

Order by writing to LifeWay Church Resources Customer Service,
MSN 113; 127 Ninth Avenue, North; Nashville, TN 37211-0113;
by calling toll free (800) 458-2772; by faxing (615) 251-5933; or by
e-mailing customerservice@lifeway.com.

**Look for other books and materials based on *How Now Shall We Live?*
from Tyndale House Publishers.**

Visit these Web sites for more information:

Charles Colson's books and tapes: chuckcolson.com
Breakpoint: breakpoint.org
Prison Fellowship Ministries: pfm.org
Other books by Tyndale House Publishers: tyndale.com

Addresses for more information:

Terry White
Communications Department
Prison Fellowship Ministries
PO Box 17500
Washington, DC 20041-0500

Public Relations
Tyndale House Publishers
351 Executive Drive
Carol Stream, IL 60188
phone: (630) 668-8300
fax: (630) 668-3245